Becoming an Outstanding Mathematics Teacher

Raising standards in mathematics is high on government education agendas and remains a key priority for schools across the country. Schools strive to provide an outstanding education for their pupils, preparing them to compete in both a national and an international market. At the heart of this is the classroom and the classroom teacher. So how do you plan lessons that engage and motivate students and what makes a mathematics lesson outstanding?

Becoming an Outstanding Mathematics Teacher aims to help teachers develop approaches to teaching and learning that take into account individual students' needs and abilities to best facilitate learning. Taking a fresh approach, it offers a wide range of techniques for planning lessons that allow teachers to use current resources (including themselves) in a more innovative way to produce outstanding results.

With a strong focus on activating learning and supporting pupils as they connect mathematical concepts and processes and develop their individual learning journeys, the book covers:

- a step-by-step approach to planning for learning
- assessment for learning and planning for progress
- developing effective questioning strategies to promote thinking skills in pupils
- techniques for differentiation to ensure all pupils make progress
- using the classroom environment to develop a culture of learning.

Packed full of practical strategies and activities that are easy to implement and including sample lesson plans, this timely new book is essential reading for newly qualified and experienced mathematics teachers who want to ensure outstanding teaching and learning in their classrooms.

Dr Jayne Bartlett has worked in education for over ten years in a range of schools with roles at senior leadership level and is currently working as an independent teaching and learning trainer and consultant.

Becoming an Outstanding Mathematics Teacher

Jayne Bartlett

Routledge
Taylor & Francis Group

LONDON AND NEW YORK

First published 2014
by Routledge
2 Park Square, Milton Park, Abingdon, Oxon OX14 4RN

Simultaneously published in the USA and Canada
by Routledge
711 Third Avenue, New York, NY 10017

Routledge is an imprint of the Taylor & Francis Group, an informa business

British Library Cataloguing in Publication Data
A catalogue record for this book is available from the British Library

Library of Congress Cataloging in Publication Data
A catalog record for this book has been requested

ISBN: 978-0-415-83113-0 (hbk)
ISBN: 978-0-415-83114-7 (pbk)
ISBN: 978-0-203-79737-2 (ebk)

Typeset in Melior
by GreenGate Publishing Services, Tonbridge, Kent

Printed and bound in Great Britain by
TJ International Ltd, Padstow, Cornwall

To Oliver

Contents

Contents

Contents

Figures and tables

Figures

Figures and tables

Tables

Acknowledgements

I would like to acknowledge Shutterstock for the use of images and photographs.

I would also very much like to thank the team at Routledge, who have given me this wonderful opportunity and have supported me in developing and creating this book.

Most of all I thank my parents, Pauline and George (Dad, thanks for the proof reading!) who, as always, have provided incredible support, my brother David and my husband Darren, who has provided endless encouragement and supported me throughout.

Finally I dedicate this book to my wonderful son Oliver, of whom I am extremely proud and who has been so patient in my writing of this book.

Introduction

Remind yourself of your story: 'Why did you become a teacher?' and, more importantly, 'Why did you become a maths teacher?' Sometimes we lose sight of what inspired us to enter one of the most rewarding and important careers of all time: teaching. It serves us well to remind ourselves of the 'why'. Whatever your reasons and whether you are new to the profession or have been teaching for some time, as teachers we all want our pupils to achieve their full potential and to continue to develop their learning and deepen their understanding and love of mathematics.

This book is the result of many years of teaching, leading departments, working as part of senior leadership and working with teachers to help them improve their practice. I wanted to write a book that focuses specifically on developing teaching and learning in mathematics. One of the main problems with whole school delivery of 'outstanding' is that it is too general. Taking generic pedagogy and translating this directly to the maths classroom, this book focuses on:

- making connections in mathematics
- developing the maths lesson
- demonstrating progress in learning
- key techniques for questioning
- assessment for learning
- differentiation
- the classroom environment
- planning for learning.

The aim of this book is to provide lots of ideas and activities that are tried and tested to support you in achieving outstanding learning and teaching and so each chapter contains multiple different examples specific to mathematics that can be used in the classroom with ease. This book is not meant to be prescriptive; after all, one outstanding teacher can teach very differently to another and no one can tell you what is going to work best for you, but having different strategies at your fingertips and exposure to lots of different ideas can really help. That's what this book is all about: providing different resources to help you to become an outstanding mathematics teacher.

The book begins by looking at what it means to be an outstanding teacher and the qualities of an outstanding lesson. Outstanding learning supports connections in mathematical concepts and processes and Chapter 1 discusses the importance of making connections. It looks at the criteria for outstanding learning and outstanding teaching, criteria that are further explored throughout the various chapters.

We normally make up our minds as to whether we are going to like something or not within the first few minutes. Chapter 2 looks at the start of the lesson and how we engage minds from the moment the students enter the classroom. It provides suggestions for a series of different activities and different ideas for structuring the start of the lesson and looks at how we set learning outcomes and begin to set a benchmark from which to measure pupil progress.

Chapter 3 looks at the main body of the lesson and how we sequence, activate and develop independence in learning while maintaining a balanced level of teacher input. It focuses on activities and ideas for introducing mathematical concepts through a learner-led approach, moving the role of the teacher to a facilitator of learning. Different teaching techniques, learning styles, cross-curricular opportunities and measures of pupil progress are discussed.

In Chapter 4 we emphasise the importance of the end of the lesson as a final opportunity to reflect on learning, to consolidate learning and to demonstrate pupil progress. We emphasise the importance of careful planning and explore a variety of different techniques through activities that allow teachers to be confident in producing an outstanding final assessment or plenary.

Chapter 5 focuses on questioning and on the importance of you as a resource in the classroom. One of the common issues is that generic terms (and whole school training), such as 'Bloom's taxonomy', are rarely translated into hierarchical questions that relate to mathematics. In Chapter 5 we take each level of questioning (from lower order through to higher order) and provide multiple mathematical examples that will support you in developing your questioning technique. Further, we take different mathematical topics and look at how we can use questioning to activate and facilitate learning.

Assessment for learning is a key feature of an outstanding lesson and Chapter 6 looks at this aspect of the lesson in detail, and on the importance of quality. It supports the teacher in using assessment for learning to drive the development of mathematics and looks at how we know pupils are making progress in our lessons. We discuss the use of learning outcomes and of giving pupils target grades or levels. Different styles of marking are discussed and examples of feedback to pupils are illustrated. Assessment strategies are highlighted throughout Chapter 6.

Developing techniques using a variety of activities or approaches to ensure that all learners make progress is important. In Chapter 7 we discuss how encouraging pupils to take ownership of their own learning can impact significantly on their engagement. Differentiation is a key topic and in this chapter we explore different types of differentiation and provide mathematical examples for each strategy.

The classroom is a multisensory environment. Chapter 8 focuses on the importance of the learning climate and how a teacher can develop a culture of learning in their classrooms even in the most challenging of schools. The correct atmosphere is very important to ensuring that learning takes place. Lots of practical suggestions are offered. We also look at the role of the classroom assistant in best supporting learning and at using the outdoor environment to enhance learning with some ideas that can be used with ease.

Chapter 9 pulls it all together and looks at developing complete lessons using the ideas and techniques discussed in the book. A variety of topics are used to demonstrate ideas for developing learning and lessons. Multiple examples and suggestions are given in this chapter. The focus is on planning for learning.

In summary, Chapter 1 looks at the criteria for outstanding teaching and learning and Chapters 2–4 look at integrating these into the lesson itself and on how to sequence and connect learning to develop an outstanding lesson through focused activities. Chapters 5–8 look at different generic pedagogies and translate these into mathematical ideas and activities that can be integrated into the sequence of the lesson to activate learning. Chapter 9 then combines all of these strategies and gives examples of how to plan for learning. While the book targets those teaching at secondary level the ideas and themes can easily be translated to those teaching pupils in the primary phase (mainly those teaching at Key Stage 2).

Overall, the book takes different aspects of pedagogy common to outstanding lessons and transforms each into a multitude of mathematical activities with ideas on how to adapt and implement them in the classroom. It is these activities and ideas that give you a platform from which to develop and combine different pedagogies to become an outstanding mathematics teacher.

CHAPTER 1

Making connections

Maths at school generally has an image of being a boring and difficult subject that has little relevance. We must ask ourselves why. Maths is one of the most engaging and relevant subjects and infiltrates all of our lives in so many ways. Yet it has a negative image among many. Consider, for instance, the response you get when you tell people you are a maths teacher. Most likely you have heard said more than once 'I could never do maths at school' or 'I hated maths at school, I was never any good at it'.

For many maths is a closed door and for some reason as a society we accept this 'can't do' or 'I'm no good at maths anyway' culture. Parents often reinforce and perpetuate this with comments such as 'it's no good asking me, I was never very good at maths either'. Maths is seen as boring and difficult and pupils can't see the relevance in their current or future lives. It is our role as teachers to try to change this image. What do pupils think about maths in your school? It is interesting to canvass their opinion. Pupils are, after all, the customers so we should really gather their feedback.

When you think about other subjects they bring learning alive with experiments, role play and media, for example. Science brings theory to life through experiment or real-life context. History is communicated through poetry, discussions, descriptions, art, dance and role play. They use different artefacts, costumes, visit different places and try to bring history alive. Maths, in contrast, is typically classroom bound and none of the above. Yet it doesn't have to be. Walk around your mathematics department at different times of the day. What do you see? Do you see pupils actively engaged in learning? Do you see pupils working together? Do you see pupils engaged in discussion or the teacher talking? Do you see pupils working individually through textbooks or worksheets? Do you see the teacher at the board demonstrating or pupils investigating? What you see is important because it will reflect the diet that pupils are receiving.

Maths is so often delivered and taught through a series of facts which pupils must memorise for a test, recall and then use. Does this really test their mathematical ability or their ability to recall? Maths is really about discovery, finding things out, investigating, making mistakes and trying new things.

Fact has its place and is needed, but not all of the time. Pupils need to be inspired, and continually learning facts and then using them actually switches pupils off. It is not very engaging. So whenever you introduce a topic, think of how you can introduce it through investigation or by asking pupils probing questions. Make them think. Engage them. Harvest the curious nature of children and encourage them to ask 'why'. For some reason we tend to knock this out of pupils as they get older!

What makes a lesson outstanding?

Achieving 'outstanding' status is something most teachers strive for (whether they admit it or not), yet few seem to achieve. So what makes a lesson outstanding and, more importantly, what does outstanding learning look like? Listed below are key features of outstanding learning and outstanding teaching (based upon the descriptors detailed in OFSTED 2012b).

In an outstanding lesson pupils are able to:

- make connections within mathematics
- show an understanding of mathematical concepts
- justify answers and discuss their ideas with their peers, demonstrating a good grasp of language and terminology
- use and apply mathematics in different contexts
- persevere with problems and adapt their approach
- demonstrate a depth of understanding
- communicate mathematics verbally and through written methods
- recognise and learn from their mistakes
- embrace new challenges with passion and commitment
- work independently and think for themselves
- recognise progress and how to achieve the 'next step'.

In an outstanding lesson a teacher:

- develops learning so that all pupils make progress
- develops pupils' conceptual understanding

- enables pupils to make connections
- knows the pupils and their learning needs
- ensures activities and tasks carefully match the learning needs and learning styles of the pupils to allow all pupils to access mathematics
- differentiates activities and strategies for delivery to optimise outcomes
- uses a variety of innovative and imaginative resources to inspire, engage and challenge pupils
- links to other subjects and to suitable real life or meaningful contexts
- uses higher-order questioning to develop learning and promote discussions
- listens and addresses misconceptions
- encourages independence
- embeds problem solving and investigation
- encourages a deeper understanding
- has high expectations of all pupils and of themselves
- uses assessment of/for and as learning
- adapts the lesson if assessment demonstrates a directional change in learning
- creates a safe and purposeful environment
- is passionate and knowledgeable about mathematics
- uses effective classroom management strategies
- uses technology where it will best impact the learning.

In this book we look at how you can be outstanding in your lessons and ensure that outstanding learning is taking place, not just for an observed lesson but as a well-established everyday learning experience for pupils. The ideas in this book are not meant to be prescriptive but offer a model about which you can scaffold and develop your own teaching and ideas.

Remember, you really are your best resource. Do you convey mathematics in a positive light? Are you enthusiastic and motivational? Do pupils look forward to learning in your lessons? Do you think about your audience? Do you think about how your learners learn when you plan your lessons?

Putting your learners at the heart of your planning is pivotal. Delivering the same lesson with the same resources year after year is not planning for learning. The lesson may have worked extremely well with one group, but may fail miserably with another. When you develop a lesson, think about how you are going to plan for learning rather than how you plan to teach.

The learning journey

We never stop learning. Whether we like it or not learning really is all around us. Learning is a journey and not always that beautiful smooth scenic route we wish it was, but often a bit of a bumpy ride taking lots of different turns (wrong and right) and changes of direction. We all learn differently, although some of us similarly, and we all learn at different rates.

Each individual lesson or series of lessons can be thought of as a learning journey. We know the end points and we know that pupils might reach them in different ways and at different times. Our role as teachers is to facilitate the learning so that we enable all pupils to make progress towards those outcomes. Indeed progress and progression in learning are addressed throughout this book.

The starting point is to think about the learning outcomes themselves and then how you are going to develop a lesson that allows pupils to achieve them. Focus on learning, not teaching. What will the starting point be? How do you know? What activities will you use to encourage pupils to think and to engage them in the learning? What is your role?

One of the most important things is to pitch the learning at the right level. Know your pupils and their learning styles. How are you going to create a lesson in which their learning is optimised with opportunities for them to work together, think and develop independently? Once you know the start point and the end point (what you want pupils to achieve) you can begin to develop a sequence of activities or problems that support this. For each activity you develop imagine yourself as the learner. Would the activity be clear to you and support progression?

Your role and working to finely balance your input are essential. Too much teacher-led input creates a passive learning environment, one in which learners become 'spoon-fed' and expect to be told something and then they follow the recipe and answer questions. A fine balance to guide the learning carefully using your input where necessary, but not to direct, is perhaps best.

Once you have completed your lesson evaluate it. Be your own critic and determine what went well and what didn't go so well. This is how we develop. Think about how you might adapt an activity that perhaps didn't have the desired outcomes. Why didn't it work? What was your input? What was the input from pupils? How did the activity develop?

Teaching can be isolating. Once you have completed your training and are in your classroom you are mostly the only adult in the room for the majority of the day and, effectively, your own boss. Monitoring is typically limited to two or three observations a year (perhaps fewer) and these observations are rarely followed up with any continued professional development (CPD). Drive your own CPD. One of the best ways to develop your teaching, in my opinion, is to observe other colleagues (and not just in your own subject) and ask other colleagues to observe you. You can focus on how they structure their lessons, how they use different activities to develop learning, how they use questioning, how they use assessment for learning, how they manage behaviour and so on. Learning from your colleagues in this way is one of the best ways to continue to improve as a teacher. Share resources; if you see a good resource then ask if you can borrow it and then adapt it as appropriate.

Finally, put yourself in the place of the learner. Would you like to be in your lesson? Is it engaging? Do you motivate your students? We often forget what it is like to be a pupil. They go from lesson to lesson, subject to subject. Do a pupil trail for half a day or a full day, if the timetable allows. Pupil trails give you great insight into the daily learning life of a pupil and will remind you that, actually, it can be quite tiring and sometimes a little boring.

Planning for learning

You have to plan for learning. This doesn't mean spending hours and putting all of your efforts into writing a lesson plan that no one will ever really look at. It means thinking how you are going to scaffold your lesson to support pupils in achieving the learning outcomes. It means carefully developing the learning journey through a sequence of well-planned activities. Never take a lesson plan done by someone else and assume it is going to fit. One size does not fit all; generic lesson plans are written by someone who is not teaching your pupils and therefore has no awareness of their learning needs or preferences. I am not keen on schemes of work that go into great detail as they dictate how topics should be taught and the resources to be used. Why? Doesn't this defeat the object of personalising learning? There is a need for knowing the topics required to be covered for a specific year group in a term (particularly if your school is assessment driven). By all means discuss ideas and share lesson plans, but always think about what is going to work for you and your learners, and if you use pre-written or prepared resources then adapt them. You are the expert and you know your pupils. If you work with them regularly to create an active learning environment rather than an 'I do, we do, you do' scenario then you will continue to observe how they learn and therefore the type of resources that will ensure they access the learning.

The first few minutes are important. This is probably where pupils subconsciously make the decision to switch off or to engage. So make sure that you pitch the initial or starter activity at just the right level, setting the scene and promoting interest. The learning should develop through the course of the lesson and the lesson should support natural progression. The rates of progress may vary but all learners should make progress. In this book I have structured the lesson into the start, main body (which has lots of subsections) and the final section of the lesson. This is not meant to be a rigid framework and, in fact, could easily have been sequenced as progressive activities. It is meant to offer guidance in developing learning.

Joining the dots and making connections

Making connections isn't just about linking with real-life scenarios or contextualised problems. It is about making connections both within and between topics in mathematics. This is important in supporting mathematical development.

Pupils are often taught discrete methods – for example, FOIL when expanding expressions such as $(x + 3)(x + 4)$ – and they fail to see connections within topics or create a real understanding of the underlying concept and what they are actually doing. They see percentages as distinct from fractions. They see solving equations as distinct from ratio. They have lists and pages of formulae and methods and attempt to memorise these for assessments. Understanding relationships is vital and making connections is so important. Why learn 30 methods if a deeper understanding enables you to learn far fewer?

How many adults or pupils are walking around with 'sine equals opposite divided by hypotenuse' in their heads because they learnt it for an exam, without having the first clue what this really means, or 'a squared plus b squared equals c squared'? You see the pride on pupils' faces when they recite these formulae, quickly lost when you ask them why. What does this mean? Why is it important? Where did it come from? How do you know? In many cases they were simply told the fact, shown when to use it and then they learnt it, with very little thinking actually involved, in fact more like following a well-rehearsed recipe.

Mathematics is so much more than learning facts; indeed, being told facts, learning them and then doing questions makes maths dull, hence so many negative opinions.

Learning through thinking?

If pupils rote learn methods then they don't really develop their thinking skills. Even the brightest can disengage and simply follow the recipe because they can and with success. However, then learners and learning become passive. We need to encourage investigation, linking mathematics, encouraging pupils to be able to select an appropriate method and equip them with the skills to be able to reason, argue and justify their decisions.

Unfortunately, in some maths classrooms there is a culture of 'I do, we do, you do', in which the teacher demonstrates the method, the class diligently follow examples, write them up and then complete 30 minutes or so of questions from a textbook. While there is a place for completing questions, as pupils do need to consolidate and practise, the issue is with the length assigned and with the delivery of the method. When introducing a concept it is important that pupils are encouraged to think and to try to develop the method independently. The role of the teacher is then to facilitate and guide this learning as appropriate. In the 'I do, we do, you do' culture we create discrete methods, which means pupils then have to rote learn methods and remember them rather than gain an understanding of the underlying mathematics.

Connecting with reality

Putting maths into context is important. Some take issue with the pseudo-reality that we often create in maths classrooms and the oversimplification of problems. I argue against this. We must introduce pupils to problems in context. It makes the mathematics interesting and engaging. Where simplification has occurred (and it will at secondary level) then discuss with pupils any assumptions that have been made and why we might make them. This is of equal importance; even the best research scientists have to make and state assumptions when modelling systems, such as epidemiologists modelling disease dynamics. The point is that they are aware of the limitations of their model and of the simplifications and assumptions that they have made. For example, in compound interest problems we make several assumptions, which of course do not necessarily reflect reality. Consider £500 invested at 2.4 per cent for three years. We assume that the money remains untouched, including the interest for the entire period. Of course, this may not be the case and this is an oversimplification of how interest is actually compounded by banks. However, as long as pupils are aware of the assumptions we have made in their model then there is no issue with the problem being simplified to this level. In fact I don't know many bankers who calculate the interest by hand and how many actually understand the underlying mathematics.

A further issue commonly raised is the use of word problems. When we use word problems one of the key concerns is that pupils tend to extract the numbers from the problem, complete the maths and then forget to put it back into context. Our role is to ensure that they re-contextualise the figures and put meaning into the mathematics and that they are able to interpret and discuss the results in the context of the question. If we can continue to encourage and expect this then pupils will naturally seek to re-contextualise. For example, on a simplistic level, if 40 people are going on holiday and a minibus holds 12 people, then how many minibuses are needed? Pupils who don't think through the problem will immediately put 3.33; however, we know in reality that we cannot have 0.33 of a minibus and so four minibuses are required.

In the following chapters we will look at how you can create lessons that are interesting and engaging for pupils. The suggestions are not prescriptive but offer guidance and ideas which you can adapt.

How does it all begin?

Imagine that you are a detective and you have arrived at the scene of a crime. First you make an initial assessment, observe the surroundings and establish the details of any witnesses. You gain their trust. You ask the right questions and listen carefully to responses. How are you going to develop the investigation? Do you need to adapt your approach? How do you know?

The start of the lesson compares with this. It sets the tone for learning and should engage pupils, capturing their interest from the outset. The very best teachers vary the techniques they use from lesson to lesson, ensuring that they carefully match any activities to their audience and use them to provide a clear assessment. The first few minutes of a lesson can serve to engage or disengage. Pupils are judging you from the moment you greet them at the classroom door. So set the tone for learning, smile and greet pupils by name and when pupils enter the classroom engage them with a short task (bell work activity) that they can complete independently until you are ready to address the class as a whole and begin the lesson.

In this chapter we focus on the importance of the start of the lesson and its role in developing an outstanding learning journey. We look at a variety of different activities and techniques that you can easily adapt and use to engage pupils, including short bell work activities, setting meaningful learning outcomes and the starter activity and its assessment.

Bell work

Very rarely do all 30 pupils arrive to your lesson at the same time and sometimes arrivals can be staggered over a few minutes. Unfortunately, if you wait for the whole class to arrive before beginning any mathematics pupils will often start talking among themselves about unrelated issues and it is then more difficult to bring them collectively back to focus. Bell work bridges this gap. It keeps those already in the classroom engaged with a short mathematical activity, emphasising mathematical purpose from the outset, until everyone has arrived (or at least the majority). You can then start the lesson when you are ready, beginning with the first learning activity.

Bell work is brief and is not a starter activity, so ideally should last no longer than a couple of minutes. It can be settling (useful if behaviour management is a concern) or active and it does not have to link to the learning in the lesson. Simple questions on the board (electronic or otherwise) as pupils arrive are a good way of continuing to reinforce numeracy. Indeed, carefully selecting the topics used for bell work and the frequency of their use can help to embed learning through repetition. Examples 2.1–2.4 are typical of bell work.

Example 2. 1
Calculate
1) -3×-4
2) 8×-7
3) -9×4
4) $-11 \times -2 \times -3$
5) $-33/3$

Example 2.3
Simplify
1) $a \times a$
2) $a + a$
3) $-b \times 3b$
4) $4c \times -4a$
5) $5m \times 2n$

Example 2.2
Calculate
1) $4 + 5$
2) $4 + -5$
3) $-3 - 7$
4) $-2 + 8$

Example 2.4
Calculate the areas of the shapes in Figure 2.1.

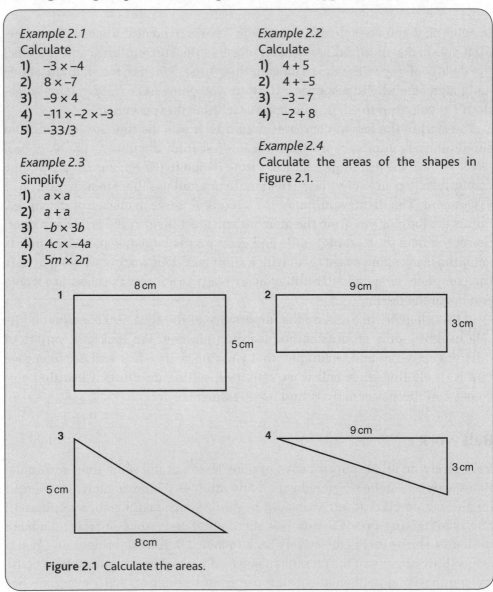

Figure 2.1 Calculate the areas.

Regular use of fractions (Example 2.5) in bell work ensures that pupils receive frequent reminders and that fractions, for example, are not kept as a discrete topic but learning is embedded through repeated practice. 'Odd one out' activities (Example 2.6) can be made as simple as you choose. You can use number (e.g. all triangle numbers except the odd one out), shape and space (e.g. images that all have rotational symmetry of order five except one image), handling data (e.g. have a box plot in the centre with the statements surrounding it all correct except one). There are lots of variations of this and the idea is to evoke mathematical thinking. As pupils leave the classroom at the end of the lesson they can go and stand by the 'odd one out' if you place cards around the room (reverse bell work). Pupils can be asked to justify their choice, promoting higher-order thinking skills.

Example 2.5
Simplify the following:
1) 16/56
2) 5/10
3) 35/45

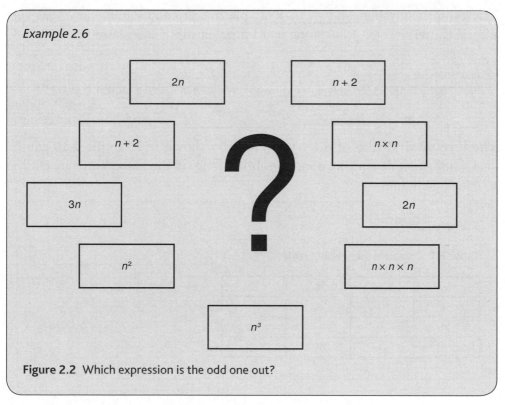

Figure 2.2 Which expression is the odd one out?

Example 2.7
If 8 × 40 = 320 then calculate
1) 0.8 × 40
2) 8 × 4
3) 0.8 × 0.4
4) 320/8

The type of bell work question shown in Example 2.8 develops manipulation of number and, used frequently (perhaps every two weeks), aids to reinforce the concept. Regular short bursts of practice help to embed learning.

Example 2.8
Make the number 24 using only 2, 3, 4

This is a nice activity as it offers natural differentiation. Some pupils may suggest simple number bonds and others more complex solutions.

The type of question shown in Example 2.9 promotes numeracy and gets pupils thinking about translating word problems into calculations.

Example 2.9
How many minutes (no calculator allowed) are there in a day, a month, a year?

The level of difficulty of the type of activity shown in Example 2.10 can be easily adjusted, depending upon the ability range of the class. You may choose to use algebra here.

Example 2.10

Table 2.1 Complete the missing values.

x		4	
		8	
7	21		35
		16	

Simple numeracy questions are useful to drop in now and again (Examples 2.11 and 2.12). Pupils often answer place value questions, such as Example 2.12 incorrectly. Using this type of question in bell work means that pupils are encouraged not only to give a numerical answer but to justify their response.

Example 2.11
Estimate the answer to the following:
1) 12.1×3.2
2) 4.8×2.1
3) 6.7×8.8

Example 2.12
Oliver says 24 is greater than 4 so 0.24 is greater than 0.4. Do you agree?

If you prefer not to develop your own bell work then there are lots of websites that have simple number challenges and can be used occasionally as a source of simple activities for bell work. Whether you use the activities or not they can be adapted and will provide you with different ideas.

Remember, since the aim is to make the bell work something pupils can be getting on with while you greet pupils as they arrive, there is no need for the mathematics to be overcomplicated. In fact, if you use bell work regularly to reinforce basic numeracy you will see an improvement in the underlying numeracy skills of pupils in your class. If settling the class is a concern, develop a routine in which the bell work is settling and is completed individually. Pupils will know what is expected of them when they arrive; that is, they open their books and begin the bell work until you are ready to collectively address the class.

Other more engaging or active bell work activities include posting a mathematical image on the board for pupils to discuss with each other, or placing images or objects around the room and asking pupils to think as they come in about mathematical connections or to place themselves by the image or object that they think is mathematically most interesting (as they leave the class at the end of the lesson they will have to justify their choice). Arguing a case and justifying choices encourages active learning. Examples are shown in Figures 2.3–2.5.

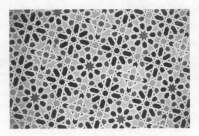

Figure 2.3 A modern office building; glazed tiles on a wall in the Alcazár of Seville; and an abstract combinatorial ornamental illustration in the style of Escher. (Images supplied by Shutterstock, www.shutterstock.com.)

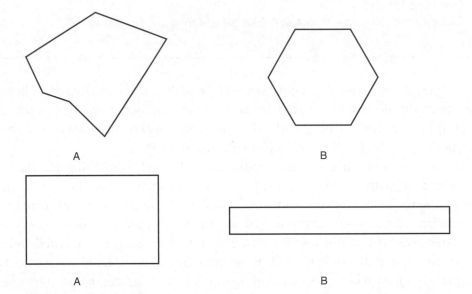

A   B

A   B

Figure 2.4 Which do you prefer? Discussion can be based around whether we are drawn to the more regular images.

Figure 2.5 What is the link between the objects in these images? Discussion can be based around rotational symmetry. Images show symmetry in nature with a five-point flower, an abstract object and a starfish. (Images supplied by Shutterstock, www.shutterstock.com.)

There is no need to review the bell work at the start of the lesson, as it is an exercise to get pupils minds into mathematics and will be returned to at the end of the lesson as pupils leave (reverse bell work). If pupils line up together outside the classroom before being allowed to enter then bell work may be unnecessary.

Learning outcomes

Sharing learning outcomes with pupils, for a lesson or series of lessons, is an important part of the learning process. If pupils can see the bigger picture and are able to see how they are going to get there and achieve the next steps in their learning then they will engage better with the learning process. They offer something by which pupils can measure their success.

Learning outcomes are not objectives. Objectives essentially become a 'to-do' list and can become very task driven. Outcomes reflect development in learning, mathematical skills and conceptualisation of mathematics. Think about the difference between the two phrases:

- 'Today I will learn to use the first law of indices …' (here the objective is to be able to use a method).

- 'Today I will develop a method for multiplying two numbers in index form …' (here the learning outcome is that we develop the method).

The first implies rote learning using a method that has been taught (often used in lessons where the teacher demonstrates and then pupils do, or 'I do, we do, you do' teaching, which will not develop outstanding learning) and the second suggests developing an understanding of the underlying process. Learning outcomes should develop higher-order thinking skills. Use Bloom's taxonomy to support this (Bloom and Krathwohl 1956). Choose verbs like evaluate, compare, solve, construct, classify, develop, examine, predict, formulate and justify, rather than 'I will know how to' or 'I will understand how to'. The UNC Center for Teaching and Learning (see http://teaching.uncc.edu/articles-books/best-practice-articles/goals-objectives/writing-objectives-using-blooms-taxonomy) has examples of verbs and questions which use Bloom's taxonomy and can help support the writing of learning outcomes.

Differentiating your learning outcomes or ensuring that pupils are aware of the range of grade criteria for a given topic is also important and they should generally cover three grades or levels to allow access for all. There is no need for pupils to write them down as this simply wastes valuable learning time. If you want pupils to have a copy of the learning outcomes or accompanying grade criteria then print them off for pupils to make reference to during the lesson as a way of evaluating their progress in learning. Bear in mind that grading outcomes can be quite controversial: fantastic if you are working with a high-achieving class, but perhaps not so with a low-ability class where seeing that they are working towards the lower end of the grade spectrum can potentially be demotivating. So proceed with caution and make the choice that best suits your learners. Key is having outcomes which develop clear progression in learning, so that pupils recognise when they are achieving success and taking those next steps.

Take the opportunity to highlight key mathematical words and vocabulary through the learning outcomes. Use the correct mathematical terms and insist that pupils do this. Literacy in mathematics is important. Very often pupils lack the ability to use mathematical language and this is often because we as educators have not stressed the importance of using the correct terminology during explanations, either written or verbal. As pupils progress in their mathematical careers this becomes increasingly important, so let's start early. Highlight key words in the learning outcomes or have a vocabulary list for each unit or topic. You would expect pupils by the end of the topic to be able to use (and I include spell here) the words correctly. There is a tendency to use 'pupil speak', but don't do this to the detriment of mathematical literacy.

Examples of learning outcomes with differentiated grade criteria are given in Examples 2.13–2.16. While examples are based on the English GCSE or Key Stage 3 (KS3) level assessment criteria, the points to note are simply the progression in outcomes. Note that the learning outcome is generic and offers a general theme for the lesson, where the grade criteria offer pupils grade-specific criteria against which to assess their own progress.

Example 2.13
Learning outcome: I will be able to develop an understanding of and apply the formula for the circumference of a circle to simple problems.

Grade Criteria:
Level 6: I will be able to:

- know and apply the formula for the circumference of a circle.

Level 7: I will be able to confidently use and apply the formula for the circumference of a circle extending to:

- calculating the circumference of an arc (semi-circle and quarter-circle only)
- using the inverse relationship.

Example 2.14
Learning outcome: I will be able to divide a quantity into two or more parts given a ratio and develop a method to check answers.

Grade Criteria:
Level 4: I will be able to:
- recognise and use simple proportions.

Level 5: I will be able to:
- use ratio notation
- reduce a ratio to its simplest form
- divide a quantity into two parts in a given ratio
- use direct proportion in simple context.

Level 6: I will be able to:
- divide a quantity into two or more parts in a given ratio
- use the unitary method.

Level 7: I will be able to:
- divide a quantity into three or more parts in a given ratio, justifying the method used.

Example 2.15
Learning outcome: I will be able to develop a method to expand and simplify the product of two linear brackets and apply to problems in context.

Grade Criteria:
Grade D: I will be able to multiply a single term over a bracket, e.g. $3(a + 2)$

Grade C: I will be able to develop a method to expand and simplify the product of two simple linear brackets, e.g. $(x - 1)(x + 2)$

Grade B: I will be able to apply the method to expand any linear expression, e.g. $(3x + 5)(2x + 3)$ or $(a - p)(2p + q)$, and justify and select the appropriate method to use in problems in context.

Example 2.16
Learning outcome: I will be able to investigate the ratio of sides of a right-angled triangle and use trigonometry in simple contexts to find missing angles.

Grade Criteria:
Grade C: I will be able to:
- use and apply Pythagoras' theorem to find the missing length
- know and use the appropriate trigonometry ratios.

Grade B: I will be able to:
- know and use trigonometry ratios and Pythagoras' theorem in combined problems
- select the appropriate method and trigonometry ratio in problem solving.

Grade A/A*: I will be able to:
- justify and explain the use of trigonometry combined with Pythagoras' theorem in 3D problems.

Some teachers prefer not to reveal learning outcomes at the start of the lesson but may slot a few minutes in at some point (and this can be the end) when they ask pupils to decide on what the learning outcomes for the lesson might be/have been and what the success criteria are/would be in achieving them and how they can take the next steps in developing learning. This is a nice activity as it encourages pupils to really think about what they have learnt and how they know they were successful in learning it. If you do choose to do this, then have a simple title at the beginning that gives pupils a flavour of what they will be studying in the lesson.

One last thing is to remember that learning outcomes are not just for pupils. Setting learning outcomes is key to planning for outstanding lessons. If you are clear on what you want pupils to achieve over the period of a lesson or series of lessons then you can work backwards from this to determine how you are going to connect a series of activities to plan a learning journey that best supports your pupils in achieving the outcomes for success.

Starter activities

The initial or starter activity is the first point of assessment during the lesson. It is the first learning activity and allows you to benchmark the pupils.

Activities can be individual, paired or grouped, but should be a maximum of about seven to ten minutes including review. If we are to develop a learning journey that allows pupils to make connections then the starter should link to the learning. It is the first activity on which we scaffold the learning.

There are plenty of different styles of starter activity and whichever you choose (and you should vary this from lesson to lesson) the most important part is the assessment and review, as with every activity that you do. So ask yourself the learning purpose of every activity. Is it a useful activity on which to build? How does it work towards achieving the learning outcomes? How does it develop pupils' mathematical skills? How does it support development in the learning journey? Has it started to lay the foundations? Asking these questions will help to ensure that progress is made. Put yourself in the place of the learner and imagine the outcomes you would expect to achieve from each activity and how they develop progress towards achieving the learning outcomes or success criteria for the lesson.

The Big Question

This is a question that asks pupils to apply their learning (see Example 2.17). Pupils are given a couple of minutes (or longer if you choose to make this your starter activity) to write down their initial response. You can make it quite fun by asking pupils to keep their answer top secret, seal it in an envelope and then return to it at the end of the lesson (sometimes the comparisons are quite remarkable in the progression they show learners have made in their own learning and for the pupils it really is tangible evidence that they person-ally have made progress). There is no need to discuss the question; this takes place at the end of the lesson and is key to assessing progress, with the aim being a question that pupils cannot answer fully at the beginning of the lesson but one they can answer at the end of the lesson following the learning phase. If you wish you can make this activity the bell work but you must ensure that all pupils have the opportunity to answer the question initially. Once pupils have attempted the Big Question (only a couple of minutes to be spent on this) we move on to the first learning activity or the starter activity. The activities so far are short (a couple of minutes for bell work, a minute or so for introducing the learning outcomes and two minutes for the Big Question) so maintaining the pace of the lesson is very important. We want initial immediate responses to the Big Question, not thought-out detailed responses at this stage.

Example 2.17

Some Big Questions:

1) What is the area of a rectangle with width $(a + 2)$ and length $(4a + 3)$?

2) Simplify:
   $5m^7 \times 3m^8$

3) Do these numbers belong in the same sequence?
   2, 5, 8, 11, 14, …
   …, 299, 302, 305, 308, …

4) Is Mr Smith the richest man in the village? (Pupils have absolutely no way of knowing the answer to this! Perhaps put up a series of images of individuals – Mr Smith may look the richest, but, following a series of mathematical clues during the lesson, is he really, or is it simply an appearance?)

5) Which horse will win the race? Images of eleven horses numbered two to twelve. Nice at the start of a probability lesson to engage pupils with the lesson; will they win? Alternatively, you can pretend pupils have £100 and they can place their bet on any of the horses (all on one or split over several). At the end of the lesson they have to decide whether their choice was a wise decision. Would they do the same again? Would they bet only on one horse if the trial was repeated? Would this be a sensible thing to do? Some lovely discussions can arise from this.

6) Kate says 'It will either rain or not rain so the probability that it will rain tomorrow is 50 per cent'.

7) Oliver says: '2 × 3 is 6 so 0.2 × 0.3 is 0.6'. Do you agree? This would precede a lesson on multiplying decimals. It is a very quick Big Question but covers a classic mathematical mistake and using it in this way ensures pupils have to justify at the end of the lesson.

8) The advert says '8 out of 10 cats prefer Whiskas'. Annie says 'I have five cats, so does this mean four of them would prefer to eat Whiskas cat food?'

9) 'Who is the most courageous?' On the board you will have images of different characters associated with the game of Top Trumps (see Figure 4.2, page 61). This is a quick decision (no more than 20 seconds) based purely on the images themselves. As the lesson progresses and pupils are given more information they can determine who the most courageous character really is.

10) 'When am I ever going to use … in real life?' This always proves interesting. At the start of the lesson you will probably get responses such as 'never', but at the end of the lesson pupils should be able to draw from their learning and think about different applications of the topic.

Benchmarking learning

So far we have used bell work to engage pupils as they enter the classroom and a Big Question that is not assessed until the end of the lesson and provides a measure of progress in learning. Both activities are relatively brief. Now it is time for an activity that allows us to benchmark the learners, ensure they have the basic skills to build on in the lesson and to identify any gaps in their learning that need addressing.

The initial activity should really make pupils think. Whether it is a series of questions that assess prior knowledge, a more investigative starter or a starter in a rich context, the important point is that we engage pupils mathematically and then involve them in the review so that they can see the value behind each activity that they do, highlighting and addressing any misconceptions. Below we discuss lots of different types of starter activities, which can be adapted and used with most topics; they should typically last between seven and ten minutes including review.

• Quick-fire questions to be completed individually can be used (Example 2.18).

Example 2.18
Indices
If $3^4 = 3 \times 3 \times 3 \times 3$

Simplify
1) $4 \times 4 \times 4$
2) $5 \times 5 \times 5 \times 5 \times 5 \times 5 \times 5$
3) $a \times a \times a \times a \times a$

Expand
4) 6^4
5) $3^4 \times 3^5$

Now simplify your answer to question 5.

Quick-fire questions involving expanding a single term over a bracket are shown in Example 2.19.

Example 2.19
Expand the following expressions and simplify where appropriate.
1) $3(a + 2)$
2) $4(b - 7)$
3) $-6(2a + 1)$
4) $-8(7 - 2m)$
5) $3(5p + 4) - 7(2p - 1)$
6) $y(2y - 3) + 2y(3y + 2)$

Such examples assess prior learning and ensure that we are aware of the baseline from which our pupils are working. This type of activity is useful in a series of lessons that build on prior knowledge and where you need to reinforce basic facts before proceeding with the main lesson. Quick-fire questions can be done with mini-whiteboards (to avoid copying use the word 'reveal' when you want pupils to hold up their boards) or individually in their books. Ensuring that pupils have a good understanding of the mathematical concepts is really the aim of this type of initial assessment activity and it is gained mainly from the review process.

- Pair-matching activities, which pupils complete in pairs or small groups, are good starter activities because they promote mathematical discussion between peers (i.e. they have to justify their choices to each other). The review is important but can be kept simple where pupils are asked to justify their 'matching pairs', or you can have each item on a piece of A4 paper and ask selected pupils to come to the front and place the correct match to form the pair. As they do so they explain their choice. Making your own are probably best as you can ensure they are appropriate for the learning needs of your class in working towards the learning outcomes. This can be an application of prior knowledge that is going to be further built on during the lesson. Examples of sources of pair-matching exercises are:

   o www.nrich.maths.org has some good pair-matching activities (electronic ones for use on the interactive whiteboard and also printable versions); for example, the multiplication challenge (http://nrich.maths.org/1252) and the coordinate challenge (http://nrich.maths.org/5038). If you search in the student section at www.nrich.org you will find lots of excellent resources at different levels of challenge.

   o Or simply make your own using, for example, Word or PowerPoint, (e.g. equivalence of decimals, percentages and fractions). Cards may have on them:

¾   0.75   0.750   75%   4/5   80%   0.8 ...

Discussion can be drawn from why we write 0.8 and not 0.80, etc. You can also use these in a 'find your partner' activity in which each pupil has a piece of laminated A4 card and they have to find their match. Making the activity more physical adds something different for pupils who may be arriving at your lesson having sat in classes for four hours or more, and it is good for kinaesthetic learners.

- 'Find the treasure' activities are engaging starters for lessons and do not solely rely on the good use of coordinates. There are many online interactive treasure maps you can use or you can simply superimpose a grid onto an image and create your own. For example, www.teacherled.com (which has lots of interactive whiteboard resources for teachers) allows you to create an interactive whiteboard map. Alternatively, borrow a few different maps from the geography department, scatter them around the room and place a transparent grid over them. You can give pairs of pupils a task that asks them to identify the coordinates of different cities or places of interest (you can have a few different cards so that not each pair has the same), or if you don't give the coordinates direct then you can create a series of problems (which can be from any aspect of mathematics) that, when solved, reveal the coordinates leading to pupils finding the location of the 'treasure' This sort of activity is just something different and pupils are often keen to solve problems to find coordinates if it leads to them finding the 'treasure' first, adding a competitive edge.

- MyMaths (www.mymaths.co.uk) has some useful interactive activities that can be used as starters. You may want pupils to do these activities individually on a computer, submit and then you can monitor scores or use them collectively as a whole-class starter activity. MyMaths is subscription based (it is good as a tool for home learning) and is useful as a tool for independent activities.

- Traditional board games are commonly used in maths classrooms. There are many adaptations; for example, snakes and ladders uses algebraic substitution. While board games are good and pupils seem to enjoy them, you must think about how you use them and what you want pupils to gain from them. To focus pupils you can ask them to write down one question on a Post-it note that they found challenging or interesting, which they can return to as the lesson develops, or you can select a few Post-it notes to review the activity as a class. Simply 'playing' a board game can be a pointless activity if pupils aren't given a task and you will find some pupils drift off task easily, but given purpose it will engage learners as you expect them to produce something from the activity.

- Bingo is another game that can be used as a starter activity, although time management can be a problem with Bingo so try to keep it brief. It is perhaps better as a plenary activity. Remember that the purpose is learning and so it is important once a pupil has got 'bingo' to review a few of the questions they got correct and involve the whole class in this process (otherwise if you focus solely on the winner other pupils quickly become disengaged). If you google 'Maths bingo cards' you will see that there are multiple editable resources available, for example, on the *Times Educational Supplement* (*TES*) website at www.tes.co.uk.

- Setting the scene through rich tasks or investigations creates a wonderful opportunity to have a more open-ended starter. They encourage pupils to develop their thinking and problem-solving skills. They can be individual or beat-the-clock team starters. Most importantly, they really engage pupils' mathematical thinking. NRICH (www.nrich.org) has some excellent tasks in rich context that can be used.

- Grid starters provide natural differentiation. They involve having a grid on the board from which you ask pupils a series of questions. As you point to the number pupils have to hold up their solution (this allows for whole-class assessment and you can select a few responses for interesting discussions). For example, in Table 2.2 pupils are told $a = 2$, $b = 3$, $c = 4$.

Table 2.2 Grid starters.

8	−4	3
2	22	5
100	14	−7

As you point to the number they either fill in their blank grid or hold up their whiteboard. For example, you point to 8. Some pupils may hold up $c + c$ or $2c$ or $4a$ or $a + c + a$ or $4b − c$. You can then talk about equivalent expressions, simplifying expressions, etc. You can adjust the level of difficulty to suit the group; for example, you may use negative numbers, e.g. $a = −3$, $b = 5$, $c = −2$. This also works well if you have iPads and Apple TV to link to your board, which enable you to show pupils the answers (mini-whiteboards are just as good as an alternative).

- Target boards are similarly useful starter activities for developing numeracy. Common examples include grids with fractions listed where questions can be of the form 'How many ways can we make four?' or 'How many ways can you make ½?' Other options include complements or grids with numbers 1 to 100 where pupils are asked to identify prime numbers, identify square numbers, identify triangle numbers, identify the factors of 35, etc. There are multitudes of ways that number grids can be used. Mike Ollerton's 'Being a Number' clip has some fun variations on the number grids (see http://www.youtube.com/watch?v=Nec3X4I33mI).

- Watching a video can be an engaging activity for pupils at the beginning of the lesson. It offers an alternative to listening to you. On the internet (e.g. www.schoolsworld.tv, www.teachersmedia.co.uk) there are several short clips relating to mathematics, for example, 'Mathematics at the mall'. Video clips can be used in so many different ways as starter activities, and, again, you need to add purpose. You can ask pupils to write on Post-it notes three key mathematical features of the clip, or you can pause the clip at key points to ask probing questions or ask pupils to predict what happens next. You may choose to return to the clip in the plenary to see if there has been development in the underlying mathematical concepts. If you google 'Marcus du Satoy' you will find he has developed some short mathematical clips that can be used in a variety of different ways in lessons.

- Websites such as www.ncetm.org.uk have some good activities that can be used as starters. Mysteries such as those shown in Table 2.3 are ideal for developing thinking skills and logic, and are good activities for pairs or small groups.

Table 2.3 Sports Day Mystery Cards (https://www.ncetm.org.uk/files/14512472/Sports+day+-+cards.pdf).

Chris, Joe, Lee and Mel are competing at their local sports day	Work out who entered which event, which house they represent and their time	The houses are named after famous sea captains	Chris ran his event in 25.75 seconds
Mel's time was 0.5 seconds slower than Chris's time	Lee's time was the fastest of all and 0.4 seconds quicker than Joe's time	Joe won the men's 100 m event	The finishing times for the four events are 15.02 seconds, 26.25 seconds, 25.75 seconds and 14.632 seconds
Drake collected points from the 15.02 seconds victory	Lee was a member of *Nelson*	The points from the men's 200 m went to *Chichester*	*Raleigh* was awarded the points from the women's 200 m event

- Bring in objects, for example, a packet of 80 teabags at £1.50 and a packet of 200 teabags at £3.50. Ask pupils to work in pairs or groups on which is the best buy and then get them to go and stand by the best buy. Choose a pair to talk through their method and ask others if they have things to add, debating the different methods teams have used. Similar activities can be done using mobile phone deals where pupils have to compare different deals and justify their best buy. There is a nice video starter on www.teachersmedia.co.uk

called 'Value for Money: mobile phone tariffs'. Other suggestions include using train timetables or bus timetables and basing different questions on these (for example, the quickest journey).

- 'Think of a number' are good starters; for example, I think of a number … double it and then take the square root. The answer is −3 or 3. What was the number? This type of starter is often used when introducing algebra or solving equations to pupils.

- Link using Skype or other such media to other schools or to businesses. This simply adds a different dimension to starter activities in mathematics. We are so often asked 'When am I ever going to use this?' so setting a live challenge (this can be pre-recorded if necessary) can help to contextualise the mathematics. For example, the local golf professional needs to work out the price of certain products for his sale or he needs to work out the VAT on goods. Show a few products over Skype and then as the lesson develops link back up and the golf professional can make up his signs as you speak (pupils like this as they see maths in action) and also pupils can talk through the best method to support the golf professional in his future percentage calculations. (Please check with video link-ups that your school are happy for you to do this within safeguarding regulations.) Alternatives include linking up with a university. Universities are always keen to work with schools and a link with a post-doctoral or research student or academic to set a mathematical task can often really add value and more meaning to the task itself.

- Podcasts (video and audio) are another alternative starter activity. For example, create a video of you measuring a bearing in silence and ask pupils to note what you do. They have to watch with intensity in order to spot the important points: drawing the north line, linking the points correctly, measuring in a clockwise direction from north, writing the bearing as a three-digit reference, etc. As part of the plenary you can ask pupils to make their own video on bearings. The best video can be placed on the maths zone of the school's learning platform.

- Targeted questioning is often used as a starter and throwing the cuddly toy around as you ask questions (particularly with younger years) to the pupil who is to answer is something pupils seem to enjoy and can be used to increase the pace. To ensure that all pupils pay full attention and are thinking about the question that you ask, don't throw the toy until a few seconds after you pose the question. This keeps all pupils on their toes! If the lesson continues the learning theme from the previous lesson or lessons, then use this technique to summarise previous learning rather than an exercise in a book. What did we learn last lesson? How do we know?

Give me an example? Argue the case that ...? Paul says '...', is he correct? Take care when throwing the cuddly toy (health and safety!).

- Sealed envelope tasks are popular with pupils. They can be individual, paired or group. Examples include statements or exercises that pupils have to complete to demonstrate learning, such as pair matching or sequencing exercises, for example, decimals with equivalent fractions. You can differentiate tasks in this way giving different pupils or groups different activities in their envelopes. Ask pupils to self-select based on their prior learning. If you have differentiated then don't go over everything in the review as pupils will easily become disengaged, select a few questions that offer good examples and review these to reinforce learning. These are particularly good for kinaesthetic learners as they are actively moving the cards while thinking about the mathematics.

- Taboo works well as a starter activity when you want to focus on developing descriptive and language skills. It is an old game in which pupils have to identify the hidden word without using the word itself (i.e. description only). Once the activity is complete, review as a class and ask a few to share their thoughts; for example, you can do this activity with a lesson on geometric properties of shapes. This can be a nice starter in which pupils describe the shapes to each other and they have to guess which shape is being described. It gets pupils thinking about the properties of shapes. As the lesson progresses you can return to this activity briefly and see if pupils would add to their initial description using more subject-specific mathematical language, thus developing mathematical literacy.

- 'Find the mathematical fact' is an active task where pupils are all given cards and they have to group themselves together to end up with a mathematical description, or each group is given a series of statements and they have to decide what the question was. This can be interesting and really gets pupils involved in mathematical debate, but make sure you watch the time. Again, as with previous activities, if you group pupils you can differentiate the task, giving different groups different problems to develop.

- Reviewing a mathematical blog is, again, a different type of starter activity for a mathematics lesson and develops pupils' thinking skills. In this type of activity pupils are asked to write comments in their teams or pairs as a response to a mathematical blog. They need to focus on the content and how they would develop or improve the blog, justifying the comments they make. If you then wish to start using mathematical blogs during your lessons or home learning this is a good way to introduce pupils to thinking about the quality of posts and the qualities of a good blog.

- Voting on two different podcasts or two different solutions to a problem are good starter activities for invoking thinking and debate. Which is the best and why? As learning is developed during the lesson, does their decision change? Why? This is a useful starter if you are going to ask pupils to develop a podcast during the lesson as it allows them to compare podcasts and discuss the features of a good podcast, which leads nicely into the main body of learning.

- The starter activity does not have to be the same for everyone. Flip a coin to divide the class roughly and randomly into two groups; one-half of the class does one problem and the other does another. For example, in a lesson that introduces Pythagoras:

  - draw to scale a right-angled triangle with sides 6 cm and 8 cm and measure the hypotenuse
  - using only the numbers 8, 6 and the operations +, × and square root, make 10.

  Review ideas briefly and then return to this as you develop the concept of Pythagoras during the lesson. This allows pupils to approach a problem from different angles. These can be brought together during the lesson to develop learning in the main body of the lesson.

- 'How many ways?' For example, issue square paper to pupils and ask them to decide how many rectangles they can draw with an area of 30 cm^2. This encourages pupils to think. It can be useful for a lesson on area or a lesson on factors. This offers challenge to pupils and you can add a time limit to enhance the competitive element. 'How many ways?' can be used with lots of different topics.

The list of different styles of starter activity really is endless. Here we have listed just a few that are easy to adapt and implement. Most important, remember, is how you use the starter activity and how it connects to the next phase in the learning journey. Does it provide a platform from which you can develop the lesson and learning?

Review

As with every activity that you do, review is an essential part of the learning process. It adds value to the activity. Providing pupils with the answers to, for example, a ten-question starter without discussion is not enough. Yes, it tells you how many questions they got correct out of ten, but it does not tell you whether they understood how to get there, had copied off someone else or were just lucky. Probing the learning is important. It is the time to ask why. What learning value did the activity have? What was its purpose in working towards achieving our learning outcomes? What have we learnt in doing the activity? Have we consolidated our prior learning or learnt something new? In the review you should know where all of your learners are. If they self-mark their work during the review, then ask for a show of hands at the end for marks out of ten, etc. This gives you a visual indication of the benchmark and so you know whether to move on to your next learning activity or whether you need to take some time aside to ensure any misconceptions are dealt with at this stage. Remember, don't just plough on because your lesson plan says it's time for the next activity. Outstanding teachers are flexible and they know when it is appropriate to continue with an activity or to redirect their plan.

Summary: start of the lesson

There are lots of different ways in which you can begin your lesson and outstanding teachers vary their methods. Imagine being a pupil going from one lesson to the next. If they are all the same we soon disengage. Adding variety makes pupils interested in learning. They never know quite what to expect next. Some examples of the start of the lesson include:

Bell work (two minutes)
Share learning outcomes (two minutes)
Big Question (one minute)
Starter activity (five minutes)
Review (two minutes)
    Total: 12 minutes

Share learning outcomes (two minutes)
Big Question (three minutes)
Starter activity (five minutes)
Review (two minutes)
    Total: 12 minutes

Big Question (five minutes)
Learning outcomes (two minutes)
Starter activity (five minutes)
Review (two minutes)
    Total: 14 minutes

Learning outcomes (two minutes)
Big Question (five minutes)
    Total: 7 minutes

CHAPTER 3

Learning in the main

I hear and I forget. I see and I remember. I do and I understand.

(Confucius)

Let us return to the detective analogy. The detective has formed his initial assessment, now he has to explore lots of different avenues, personalise his approach, question different individuals and groups, and really probe further in order to ensure he solves the crime and achieves his outcomes. He needs to direct the investigation based on his assessments and use different techniques to engage with the individual.

The initial assessment activity is complete and pupils know what they are working towards. This next phase of the lesson or the main body of the lesson develops, secures and embeds the learning. We all learn differently. You have 30 individual minds sitting in your classroom and 30 individual minds to engage and captivate.

In this phase of the lesson we conceptualise the mathematics and develop thinking skills: information processing skills, reasoning skills, enquiry skills, creative thinking skills and evaluation skills (perhaps not all in the same lesson!). In using these thinking skills pupils learn to learn, they learn how as well as what and in the moments of reflection they think about thinking (metacognition).

To achieve these objectives the lesson needs to be appropriately divided into different activities, each followed by a review or mini-assessment that is built into your planning. Engaging pupils with activities means that activities really need to be of an appropriate length, purposeful and challenging. An appropriate length is difficult to define (it could be five minutes, seven minutes or twenty minutes) and perhaps a better suggestion is for you to be able to judge well when the time is right to stop, regroup and assess. Are pupils starting to get fidgety? Are there questions that need to be addressed collectively? Do you need to pull ideas together? Outstanding teachers facilitate learning and they do so through a sequence of cleverly linked activities and regular reviews (or mini-plenaries). They know when to draw an activity to a close or when to pause and ask probing questions to challenge thinking or redirect learning and their lessons simply seem to flow.

Sequencing the learning

He who learns but does not think, is lost! He who thinks but does not learn is in great danger.

(Confucius)

An important part of developing pupil's skills in mathematics is correctly sequencing the learning activities. This is not to say that the lesson must follow and stick to a rigid plan. More that as you plan activities you must be thinking about how these build on one another and develop the mathematical concepts and skills needed to work towards meeting the learning outcomes. A starting point is to think about the end point and then work backwards, or to 'chunk' the learning. This approach can be extended beyond the lesson plan to the scheme of work for a series of units.

When we start to sequence the learning and develop mathematical concepts we need to ensure that we act as a facilitator of learning. We can teach pupils to pass an exam and, unfortunately, some teaching has become 'teach to the test'. However, this only goes so far and if we are to develop pupils who can compete with their peers, not only nationally but internationally, then we must develop mathematicians. To do this we need to ensure that in our lessons we are encouraging pupils to think and to develop (with our guidance) an understanding of mathematics and the connections within the subject. This creates a much more powerful learner who is able to approach problems with confidence and who can apply their knowledge. Avoid telling pupils how to do something and develop your teaching to facilitate their thinking. In other words, lets remove the 'I do, we do, you do' culture of teaching.

For example, in a lesson that involves developing an understanding of the rules of indices, you may choose to start with an activity that asks pupils to expand two expressions, multiply them and then to investigate the results, e.g.

$$5^3 \times 5^4 = 5 \times 5 \times 5 \times 5 \times 5 \times 5 \times 5 = 5^7$$

Pupils will hopefully spot the connection following a series of these questions (i.e. we add the indices).

This can be extended to division and to terms involving simple algebra, e.g.

$$a^4 \times a^2$$

As we develop the learning, subsequent activities may look at negative indices and what this means. This can be done through the relationship

$$5^3 \rightarrow 5^2 \rightarrow 5^1 \rightarrow 5^0 \rightarrow 5^{-1} \rightarrow 5^{-2}$$

and so on, where pupils see the theme of dividing by 5 therefore equates to

$$5^3 \rightarrow 5^2 \rightarrow 5^1 \rightarrow 1 \rightarrow 1/5 \rightarrow 1/5^2$$

Or, alternatively, through a method (which perhaps better sequences the learning) that builds on the previous activity, for example,

$$5^2/5^4 = 5^{2-4} = 5^{-2}$$

(using the earlier concept of subtracting the indices when we divide).

Expanding and simplifying means
$(5 \times 5)/(5 \times 5 \times 5 \times 5) = 1/(5 \times 5) = 1/5^2$
This leads to pupils understanding that 5^{-2} is equivalent to $1/5^2$.

The really important point is developing the concepts and creating an environment in which pupils discover the rules through investigation. This means pupils are not learning a method (and in this case up to three methods, i.e. add indices when we multiply, subtract indices when we divide and so on), but rather are able to understand the concept, leading to greater fluency in mathematics and an ability to make connections. We want pupils to learn 'how and why' to promote a deeper understanding. Allowing pupils to visualise and discover the mathematics is much more powerful than telling them a rule and expecting them to use it.

Let's look at the addition of fractions. Very often a method is taught to pupils that they learn, and so is consequently procedural.
For example,

$$4/7 + 6/7 = 10/7$$

When you ask pupils to explain what they are doing they often say 'add the numerators and leave the denominators (if they are the same)'. They then complete a procedure to write the fraction as a mixed number, that is, ten divided by seven is one whole one, remainder three, leaving us with 1 and 3/7. But do pupils really fully understand the concept? Can they explain what they are doing and why?

If we take a slightly different approach when we introduce fractions and build on pupils' understanding of number bonds (foundations built early in their learning), we remove the procedural element and connect the mathematics.

For example, in Figure 3.1 pupils have used their knowledge of number to split the second fraction to make one with the first. Building relationships early on can help develop greater mathematical understanding and a better ability to manipulate mathematics as a pupil progresses.

Developing a method for solving equations, for instance, can also build on the number bonds introduced in the early stages of learning. If pupils are aware of the meaning of the equals sign, for example, $2 + 3 = 5$, then if we subtract one from the left-hand side to balance the equation we must subtract one from the right-hand side.

Extending this to the notion of 'balancing' develops the first stages of solving an equation such as $4x + 3 = 9$. Making such connections between mathematics sequences the learning and links concepts developed earlier in their careers. For instance, if you ask some pupils why they subtract three, responses are such as 'you do the opposite on the other side' or 'what you do to one side you do to the other'. When you ask why, some pupils are unable to answer. If we develop the relationship between number bonds early then pupils have a natural understanding of why they are subtracting three and mathematics becomes a smooth flow and a series of connectives.

How pupils make notes during the period where the concept is developed is entirely up to you and the style of working you feel best suits the learners in your class. Indeed, for different activities this may vary. You may want pupils to note a more formal method following the deduction of the process (including any associated mathematical language or definitions) and, in addition, note their own thoughts for the method or make a pictorial representation. This is important as a reference point for pupils and should be simple and clear. Alternatively, as pupils complete the mini-assessments or challenges ask them to note carefully what they are doing and thinking at each step. This needs to be carefully checked when you mark pupils' work.

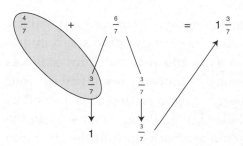

Figure 3.1 Building mathematical understanding.

Mini-assessments

As you develop mathematical concepts, if you find yourself talking then ask yourself whether you could turn this into a question that you pose to pupils in order to reach the same outcome. Sometimes we don't realise how long we have been talking for, so make your aim to facilitate rather than talk through the learning. After the introduction of each new concept add a few quick fire questions to assess pupils understanding. Bounce these from one pupil to the next rather than from pupil to you and back (use basketball rather than ping-pong questioning, i.e. pass the question around the class to develop the answer). Quick-fire questioning can be done individually and need only last for two minutes. Use mini-whiteboards to assess the whole class. For example, returning to indices after developing the first concept, you may have four simple questions, as in Example 3.1.

Example 3.1
1) $5^3 \times 5^9$
2) $a^{20} \times a^{121}$
3) $4^{-3} \times 4^3$
4) $100^0 \times 100^3$

After each question (reveal them one-by-one) confirm understanding with a few key questions. If, for example, pupils give 4^0 as an answer to question 3 you may then select a pupil who has given one as an answer to explain. Which is better and why, or doesn't it matter? If appropriate you can ask pupils to RAG rate their understanding (red, insecure; amber, okay but more practice needed; green, secure). This can then be used to support pupils in the choice they make during self-selection exercises.

You may choose to use a simple pair-matching activity or card sort and ask pupils to work through this individually, in pairs or in groups to assess understanding. There are lots of different card sorts and pair-matching activities available, but for a simple mini-assessment it is probably best to create your own to match the learning outcome you are trying to secure. This also offers a greater depth of personalisation and, indeed, not all pupils have to do the same assessment activity; for example, you may choose to split the class into two with one half doing one activity and the other doing another. This is useful when you have different styles of learner and where different activities are used to assess.

The most important outcome of a mini-assessment is that it enables you to judge whether the understanding is secure and that you can move forwards in the lesson plan. If it reveals a lack of understanding then deviate from your plan and complete further discussion or activities to ensure the learning is embedded, in other words redirect the learning. As the concept is further developed add a mini-assessment and repeat the learning cycle until you are confident that all of the mathematical concepts needed have been introduced. Mini-assessment activities act as a progress check.

The main assessment activity

Once pupils have developed an understanding of the mathematics required to secure the learning outcomes through the initial activity or series of activities, then they do need to complete the main assessment activity. There are lots of different assessment activities that embed learning and these should be slightly longer than the periods allocated to the shorter activities above, allowing pupils thinking time and time to process their learning. You will know when the time is right to draw the activity to a close for feedback and review. Quality is important here, not quantity.

The worksheet

If you choose to use a worksheet then I recommend that you have three different worksheets. Don't pre-assign pupils to these. Pupil choice is important here and the selection should be based on the outcomes of the mini-assessments. Just because a pupil is given a certain target grade or level, or because they fall in the bottom quartile of the class, or because on the previous topic they did not perform well, does not mean that they should automatically be given a worksheet that supports the weaker learners. Labelling pupils in this way can limit their progress and impact their motivation. Choice should be made based on performance on the day with a given topic combined with the outcomes of the mini-assessments. This is how we begin to challenge learning (obviously, if you know that a pupil has made an unsuitable choice then you may want to guide their selection). Try to avoid the obvious colours of red, amber and green (RAG) for the worksheets. This can really serve to demoralise those who are always red. Perhaps have sheets that lead to the same learning outcomes, but do so in slightly different ways. Change the identifiers each lesson; use letters or shapes to name the sheets and have the learning outcomes and key vocabulary on each worksheet to reinforce literacy.

If you choose to do a worksheet, how you structure the worksheet is important. In the mini-reviews you have assessed the pupils using simple questions that directly apply the knowledge, so for this main activity it is important to mix the style of questions to ensure that this activity builds on the previous one and develops pupil thinking skills further. Don't do more of the same, which doesn't show progress, but simply demonstrates that pupils can do 30 questions over five. If they can do five then they don't need to do 30 to reinforce the concept. You have already checked their understanding of the concept in the mini-review. Now is the opportunity to see if they can apply what they have learnt, which further demonstrates their understanding, so introduce some applied questions at this stage. Quality over quantity!

Some pupils may require more support with applied questions and so you may choose on one worksheet to split a question into several parts or to scaffold the question and on another to simply pose the question direct. This gives the more able pupils the opportunity to immediately apply their mathematics, and at the same time supports weaker pupils through the question. Similarly, on one sheet you may have a series of hints or have a sheet of hints prepared so that if pupils need additional support they can ask for the hint sheet. There is no problem with doing this as long as the hint sheet still encourages pupils to think. Examples taken from a quadratics worksheet focusing on expanding brackets (developed using the rectangle method) are shown in Examples 3.2 and 3.3.

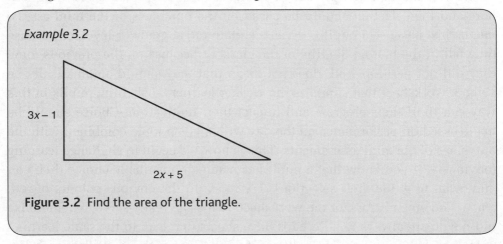

Example 3.2

$3x - 1$

$2x + 5$

Figure 3.2 Find the area of the triangle.

Example 3.3

a) How do you work out the area of a rectangle?

b) What is the area of the rectangle in Figure 3.3?

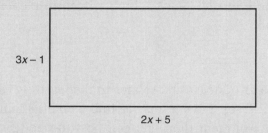

Figure 3.3 What is the area of the rectangle?

c) Can you use this information to find the area of the triangle in Figure 3.4?

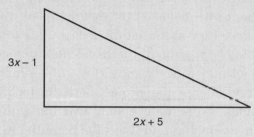

Figure 3.4 Find the area of the triangle.

d) How have you managed to calculate this?

Allowing pupils the choice over the questions that they complete is very important, both for a single worksheet and for multiple worksheets. Avoid working from 1 to 20 in order. You can guide this choice by having different pathways or allow self-selection.

I suggest a short period of self-marking (for one minute put answers up visually, no need for you to read them out), or alternatively use peer assessment and then select a few questions that you feel offer different applications of the mathematics to discuss as a whole class or ask individual pupils to offer feedback. You will have a very good idea of pupil performance through your circulation around the classroom as pupils are completing the activity (aim to get round all pupils). The self-marking gives an immediate quantitative summary to pupils and they are able to make comments on their own performance against success criteria using this as a guide. If pupils have any concerns or questions about this activity, then you can ask them to make a note in their book which will form part of the pupil–teacher written dialogue.

Video/podcast

Asking pupils to create a video or podcast that relates to the learning can be a very powerful learning tool. If you have a learner hub or maths zone on the school virtual learning environment then you can post the podcasts or videos on this if appropriate (quality assure them first). Mobile devices such as video cameras, a mobile phone with video capacity or iPad are excellent for creating videos (dependent, of course, on your school usage policy and opinion on pupils bringing in their own devices). There are lots of websites or apps where you can create videos from assimilation of clips. It is probably worth liaising with your technology department for ideas and video-editing software packages that the school may already subscribe to. Alternatively, you may want to make this a cross-curricular project between technology and mathematics. What video does is offer an excellent way for students to develop their creative skills in mathematics and it has the potential to really engage pupils (e.g. Example 3.4).

> *Example 3.4*
> 1) Create a video for the local junior/infant school (if the video quality is good these can actually be sent to and used by the local schools) on a particular aspect of mathematics – perhaps fractions, transformations or simple algebra.
> 2) Create a video for a non-mathematician on calculating percentages or VAT or percentage profit or loss.
> 3) Create a video for revision to be posted on the school website; each group could be given a different topic and then these can be shared among the class for revision purposes. Quality control is obviously important. This may take longer than one lesson or may be a joint project with the ICT department.

Limit the videos to five or so minutes and ensure you are familiar with the software and any other tools yourself. A good idea is to create a 'Here's one I did earlier' video to demonstrate to pupils the quality you would expect.

Ask pupils to critique your video (this could be a starter activity) and then allow them planning time for their own before they get to work. Where pupils are working in small groups, allocate particular roles. One final note is that pupils really enjoy watching the videos and sharing their work, so make sure you leave time for this (this would probably form the start of the next lesson). The video can form part of an assessment opportunity, particularly if assessing personal learning and thinking skills.

Computer activities

There are numerous mathematics computer applications and if you are setting a computer activity during the lesson then ensure that it serves a purpose. Set pupils an initial challenge. Don't just make it about sitting at the computer and completing a few questions. This can lead to some pupils becoming disengaged with the activity as they are unsure of the success criteria or they simply drift off-task. Always ensure that there is an associated learning outcome. You may choose to set a series of questions that pupils need to answer following the computer task. For example, if you are completing questions on bearings, then ask pupils to note down one of the questions and do a diagrammatic representation of how they interpret the question and how they may solve the problem with a written method, noting any key concepts. Or have a question pre-prepared on a sheet that pupils need to work through applying the skills and knowledge they have learnt during the computer activity. Many of the websites, such as MyMaths (www.mymaths.co.uk), are subscription based, but as part of this have tracking systems to allow you to monitor pupil performance, which is a useful tool.

Using graphing software such as Autograph (www.autograph-maths.com) is excellent for investigative style activities. For example, if you want pupils to investigate simultaneous equations graphically or investigate the effects of m and c in the equation $y = mx + c$, where plotting on paper can take a very long time (and an exercise in plotting graphs is perhaps a different lesson), packages such as Autograph can lead to immediate visualisation, allowing the focus to be on the learning outcomes and letting pupils really investigate the mathematics (i.e. the effects of the gradient and y-intercept). You could ask pupils to identify the odd one out of a series of four equations and to explain why

$$y = 3x + 2 \qquad y = 3x - 5 \qquad y = 10 - 3x \qquad y = x - 5$$

This encourages pupils to compare and contrast different features of the straight-line graphs. They then have to justify their answer, which leads naturally to investigating the features of $y = mx + c$ and the effects of changing m and c on the straight-line graph. This gives a real purpose to the activity. In other words, they are not just playing around on the computer until you say time is up.

Activities like this can be easily differentiated and personalising the learning is important to ensure that all pupils can access the activity. For each aspect of the investigation set a time limit and then ask pupils to feedback. Screenshots can be taken for evidence and for their notes. Working in pairs on this type of activity can support those who are not so confident on computers and encourage discussion between peers. Autograph is also fantastic for investigating transformations. Often Autograph is an under-used resource and yet it has much to offer in supporting the investigative and visual representation of mathematics.

Geometer's Sketchpad (www.dynamicgeometry.com) is also an excellent resource. It is a useful tool for independent learning, for example, deriving circle theorems. GeoGebra (www.geogebra.org) is also a good package and it is free. It offers interactive graphics, algebra and spreadsheet facilities. Suffice to say, there are many other excellent software packages available. As with all computer packages, familiarising yourself with the software and being clear on the learning outcome, timing the task so that it is efficient and pupils don't drift off task, is important to make the task relevant and to ensure that the use of computers in your lesson becomes a powerful learning tool.

Textbooks

Textbooks, if used well, can be a good resource. Where they fail is when they form the majority of the main assessment activity or the majority of the lesson, or where they become your main teaching tool. Teaching a topic and then asking pupils to turn to a page and complete an exercise from the textbook does not enhance the learning experience. While it is true that many have fantastic professional illustrations and diagrams, textbooks are generic teaching tools and can be a challenge when personalising learning. If you are using textbooks, then don't use them all of the time (as this becomes tedious for pupils) and when you do use them select the appropriate section first and identify different pathways for pupils. Typically, more applied questions come at the end of the exercise or as an extension activity, but if you start at the beginning and work through many pupils do not reach these more open, thought-provoking questions. Ensure that all pupils have the opportunity to try them. For example, you may ask pupils to complete two questions from section A, three from section B and then the extension activity. As with the worksheets, encourage self-differentiation and allow pupils to choose the questions that they complete. I personally don't use textbooks with classes as I like to create more personalised resources, but do use them as a source of different ideas.

Rich tasks

Rich tasks can enable pupils to:

- explore mathematics using a variety of different methods in intriguing contexts
- pose as well as solve problems, make conjectures
- extend knowledge or apply knowledge in new contexts at a range of levels
- broaden their problem-solving skills and deepen their mathematical content knowledge
- reveal underlying principles or make connections between areas of mathematics.

Investigations are an important part of developing higher order thinking skills in mathematics and there is a genuine need for a balance between content- and process-based learning outcomes. Rich tasks can be used in a variety of ways. Some prefer to use them at the start of a topic to develop discussion and promote a 'what have we learned' culture and others prefer to use them at the end of a topic to assess how well pupils can apply the knowledge that they have acquired. You may choose to set a rich task as an open plenary activity that is continued for home learning and discussed at the start of the next lesson. It may form part of an extended mathematical project for home learning – www.nrich.org has lots of examples of rich tasks and how they can be extended, such as in Example 3.5.

Example 3.5
Number pyramids. Pupils are asked to spot the relationship between consecutive layers in the pyramid (adjacent numbers are added). Various questions are posed. What happens to the top number if the bottom numbers are changed? Can you express the solution algebraically? An example of the pyramid is shown in Figure 3.5.

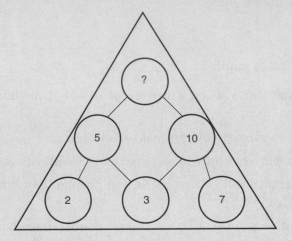

Figure 3.5 Number pyramid.

Marbles in a box. Imagine a three-dimensional (3D) version of noughts and crosses in which two players take it in turn to place different coloured marbles into a box. The box is made from 27 transparent unit cubes arranged in a 3-by-3-by-3 array. The object of the game is to complete as many winning lines of three marbles as possible. How many different winning lines are there?

Painted cube. Imagine a large cube made up from 27 small red cubes. Imagine dipping the large cube into a pot of yellow paint so the whole outer surface is covered, and then breaking the cube up into its small cubes. How many of the small cubes will have yellow paint on their faces? Will they all look the same? Now imagine doing the same with other cubes made up from small red cubes. What can you say about the number of small cubes with yellow paint on?

How many chickpeas does it take to fill the room? In this investigation provide pupils with a variety of measuring instruments (e.g. trundle wheel, metre rule, measuring tape) and with a bag of chickpeas each and have smaller cuboid containers around the room. How are we going to begin (allow pupils five minutes planning time in small groups)? How might we find the volume of the room? How might we find the volume of one chickpea? Is there a better way? What assumptions have we made? How accurate are our measurements? There are lots of ways in which this investigation can be extended and developed and it is a good way of using and applying volume, accuracy, measure and calculation.

Working together

Learners retain 90 per cent of what they learn when they teach someone else, compared with 10 per cent of what they learn when they read. Working together, whether as a pair or in a group, supports cooperative learning. Almost any activity can be turned into a group activity or a paired activity. There can be value in grouping pupils close in ability and at times grouping pupils who are different in their abilities. You must choose this sensibly based on the activity you are doing and the outcomes you wish to achieve. One thing that is advisable is that you mix pairings or groups each lesson or series of lessons so that pupils become used to working with different pupils on a regular basis and know that you select the groupings rather than them.

Discussed below are different types of group activities.

Jigsaw

Each pupil is given a different piece of information and when the group comes together they piece together the information to complete the 'jigsaw'. An alternative to this is that each group is a piece of the jigsaw and when the class is pulled back together the work from each group is joined to complete the picture. Another idea is that pupils within a group are numbered (e.g. one to five). All of the pupils numbered one form a new expert group, all of the pupils numbered two form a new expert group, and so on. In the newly formed expert groups they focus on a specific aspect of mathematics or problem. After a given period the original groups are reformed and pupils numbered one to five teach their findings back to the original group one by one. This works well with a variety of different problems (e.g. a series of different applications of Pythagoras).

Think, pair, share

Think, pair, share is effectively a cognitive rehearsal structure. The idea is that you pose a problem and allow all pupils to think individually for a short period, they then discuss their findings in pairs and then further share these in groups or as part of a whole-class discussion. This can be used for all activities. It is particularly useful as a tool for developing confidence in learners, where they are more likely to make suggestions if they have had their thoughts affirmed by another pupil.

Carousel

In the carousel each group moves from one activity to another. This can be used in lots of different ways. Each group can have a different coloured pen and can be asked to add to the previous groups contributions to a problem, or each group can contribute independently to each problem and at the end the different solutions can be compared and discussed. If you wish to assess the activity, you can station yourself at one point in the carousel so that you can observe how each group approaches one particular problem.

A nice carousel activity is one in which pupils are given questions with a solution that has a misconception and they are asked to identify the error and then offer a correct response. To ensure that groups remain focused add the 'race against time' element and time the activities, for example five activities at three minutes each. Change the roles (e.g. the scribe on each rotation) so that all pupils take on different roles during the activity (this can be done easily by numbering pupils within the group and on each new activity a different number becomes, for example, the scribe). Other activities include introducing a real-life application of the mathematics and problems to which pupils are asked to contribute. The activities can embrace different learning styles; one problem may involve structuring a model, another creating visualisation of the mathematics through diagrammatic representation and another writing a contribution to a Twitter feed.

Speed dating

This is another fast-paced activity and involves half of the class remaining in their seats and the other half of the class hot-seating and moving each time the bell is rung. Give each pupil in the class a card with a problem on it. They have a few minutes to become an expert on this problem. Make sure you have written the solution to the problem on the back of each card and after a few minutes ask pupils to turn over and compare their solution with the one on the card. Respond to any questions. Now the speed dating starts and pupils are given one minute with a partner to teach the solution to their problem and vice versa. Pupils use a Post-it note to record any really good contributions to their own problem and then also any questions they have about other problems. As the speed dating progresses pupils become more confident with their own problem and are exposed to other problems. At the end of the event ask pupils to write up a solution to their own problem with any key questions that were raised. These can be posted on www.docs.google.com or Wallwisher as a homework activity that you can review. Following review they can be posted on the virtual learning environment.

As this can take quite a lot of time an alternative is to only have six questions. Form groups initially of six and allow pupils in each group to become experts on the problem. Pupils then pair with pupils from another group, for example all pupils in group one pair with a pupil from group four and they challenge them with their problem or teach their solution to the other pupil and then swap after a minute. This makes the activity shorter and allows you to ask each group to reform and then after five minutes of noting any comments they have received from the speed dating activity to produce a presentation of their problem and solution to the class.

Independent learning

Building mathematical confidence comes through the development of independent learning skills. Pupils need to learn how to learn and much research has been done in this field. The purpose here is not to delve into the theory but to look at how we can use independent learning techniques to support mathematical learning. There needs to be a shift from the dependent learner to the independent learner and if you are keen to develop independent learning in your classroom, department and school then start early because as pupils progress through school they will move along the spectrum of learning and become more independent.

So what does the phrase 'independent learning' actually mean? Well, independent learning is where pupils become involved in their own learning experience. Pupils are actively encouraged to think for themselves and reflect on their learning and setting targets, as appropriate.

In outstanding lessons 'Pupils show exceptional independence and take the initiative in solving problems in a wide range of contexts, including the new or unusual. They think for themselves and are prepared to persevere when faced with challenges, showing a confidence that they will succeed' (OFSTED 2012a).

The activities we have discussed in Chapter 2 and in this chapter all promote independent learning.

Individual learning preferences and mathematics

There are three primary channels through which we learn: visual (through sight), auditory (through sound) and kinaesthetic (through touch). Some individuals learn through a mixture of these media and for others one particular learning style dominates. Think about your lessons. Do you mix it up? If there was a learner with a strong kinaesthetic preference would they be able to access your lessons all of the time? Do your activities support different learning styles? Often our day is so hectic that we don't have time to think explicitly about learning preferences on top of everything else, but simple techniques can ensure that each activity you do can be accessed by all learners.

Examples of kinaesthetic activities

Investigations

Set up some investigations that involve pupils physically 'doing'. For example, you may have a series of triangles scattered around the room for investigating trigonometry or have some counters on the table for investigating ratio or use oranges for investigating the surface area of a sphere. The 'oranges activity' is a nice activity for kinaesthetic learners because more often than not pupils are told formulae, whereas this activity allows them to investigate. Ask pupils to draw circles around a large orange (the idea being that the radius of these circles is the radius of the orange. If they struggle here they may have to cut the orange in half (or for health and safety perhaps you should do this) and then use acetate which can be wiped clean. Then ask pupils to peel the orange (smallish pieces) and stick the pieces of peel in the circles. The idea is that pupils will fill four circles, leading to them determining that the surface area of a sphere is 4 × area of a circle (or $4 \times \pi \times radius^2$). This really engages kinaesthetic learners. The key is to encourage pupils to translate these activities into language so that they can explain the mathematics through demonstration.

Getting up

Allow pupils to come to the board to demonstrate solutions or try to embed the sense of mathematics in movement. For example, you may ask half of the room to stand up and turn 90 degrees clockwise and the other half to turn 270 degrees anticlockwise. Are they facing the same direction? Why? Ask five boys and ten girls to stand up. Ask the girls to move next to a boy so that standing next to each boy is the same number of girls. Talk about ratio and 1:2. Develop ratio further using this technique.

Probability lines are another good option with kinaesthetic learners. Have a line from zero to one and ask pupils to place mathematical language along the line (for example certain, equally likely, etc.), and then ask them to place a series of events on the line. Place pupils in order of height and then talk about the middle value. Have an image of a mouse or a small soft toy, for example, and ask where that would go. This can lead to a nice discussion as to whether the median is affected by extreme values. You can then do a calculation on the mean height (before and after including the mouse). Trying to embed mathematics in this way will help a kinaesthetic learner.

Card sorts or pair matching activities

These are good for engaging the kinaesthetic learner as they are actively doing something (i.e. physically moving cards with their hands while thinking) while at the same time having to think about the mathematics. Figure 3.6 shows an example of simple pair-matching cards that can be cut up for pupils to match together.

$3(a+2)$	$3a^2 + 3a$
$7(2a-8)$	$-8a + 12$
$8(2a-1)$	$-15a + 15$
$5(-3a+3)$	$14a + 56$
$7(2a+8)$	$16a - 8$
$-4(2a-3)$	$3a + 6$
$3a(a+1)$	$15a - 15$
$5(3a-3)$	$14a - 56$
$-7(2a-8)$	$-16a - 8$
$-8(2a+1)$	$-14a + 56$

Figure 3.6 An example of a simple pair-matching exercise.

Examples of visual activities

Drawings

Expressing mathematical connections in drawing is a powerful tool for visualising the mathematics as a series of pictures. For example, dividing £300 in the ratio 2:3. Pupils may draw a diagram splitting £300 into five equal-size piles. Each pile will contain £60. They will then be able to make the connection that two piles are worth £120, and so on. The diagrammatic nature of this reinforces their learning.

Mind mapping

This is a very good way of allowing pupils to visualise mathematics, and is very good for revision purposes. You could prepare cards which, when put together, form a mind map, and ask pupils in pairs to complete the diagram. This allows for kinaesthetic learning as well.

Interactive whiteboard

This is a good way to demonstrate mathematics to a visual learner, and actively asking pupils to come to the board and interact with an activity also embraces the kinaesthetic learner.

Example of auditory activities

Peer hearing

Let pupils read to each other. Allow them to read, for example, their method for solving a problem. Listening to each other helps auditory learners develop their language skills.

Podcasts

Pupils become the maths 'expert' where they explain mathematics for the purposes of a podcast. This will help to embed their understanding.

Real-life meaning

Link the mathematics to real-life connections in your explanations.

Linking with other departments

This has to be one of my favourite aspects of mathematics. Developing cross-curricular links adds value to learning and offers a different dimension. Far too often mathematics is divorced from anything meaningful to pupils and taught in its own discrete world. I would imagine that once in your career (and most likely more) you have heard a physics teacher make a comment along the lines of 'they just can't rearrange formulae and do basic mathematics'. You feel like showing them the beautiful pages in the pupils' maths books of perfectly rearranged equations. What we are really saying is that they cannot transfer the skill from mathematics to the contextualised skill in physics (or that in physics they try to instil a different method, which confuses pupils and serves only to create further distinction between the subjects and, more importantly, methods for rearranging equations). The very best teachers make connections and relate maths to other areas. Below I offer a few easy-to-implement ideas (and there are so many more) for simple cross-curricular links that are effective and easy to establish because mathematics really is everywhere. This does not have to be something that is restricted to younger pupils. Indeed, there are some wonderful ideas at http://plus.maths.org that challenge pre-university pupils. It is important to create these links and to start talking with other departments because it is essential that teachers of other subjects are aware of basic numerical methods learned in mathematics. Numerical consistency across subjects is vital in raising standards.

Maths and design technology

If you are completing a unit on ratio then why stick to a maths classroom? In a lesson combined with design technology (DT) add an interesting activity. Get pupils baking cakes or other simple quick-to-cook recipes. You can provide pupils (in pairs) with different recipes for cakes, for example give them a 'serves twelve' recipe and ask them to work out the recipe for 'serves eight'. This is a nice activity because you can challenge the more able by mixing units of measure and by making the ratios more complicated and simplify for those who require further support, but all pupils are actively involved in the lesson and all pupils get to make the cakes. The starter activity can be based on getting the right ratios and then following a mini-review they can get cooking. The plenary can be a demonstration of their cakes and pupils can be asked to write a story board for simplifying ratios or finding equivalent ratios, or use the time the cakes are baking for pupils to use shape and space to design the cake container.

Other lessons with DT include scale drawings. If you are working on scale then team up with a design lesson and add that practical dimension. Take the maths lesson to the DT lab and use the computer-aided design packages to support the learning. Set a problem between you and DT that will enhance both subjects and allow pupils the freedom to investigate. The mathematics can be continued in the mathematics lesson and the design element in the DT lesson. Joint planning in this regard also ensures that numeracy across the curriculum is consistent (i.e. non-maths specialists are delivering mathematical content with the correct mathematical processes).

Maths and science

This is the obvious subject to link with mathematics and there are lots of rich examples of mathematics in science. What really is important when there are such close links is that the mathematics used in science follows the correct mathematical procedures so that pupils are not learning, for example, a particular technique in science for plotting a scatter graph and a different technique in maths. So liaison between departments is very important.

Cross-curricular opportunities are very diverse with science. They can be as simple as conducting an experiment and then using the results in a mathematics lesson that focuses on handling data. They can extend to the physics of forces and resolving forces in mechanics.

A fun activity is the rocket design project, where pupils get to make a rocket out of various materials and then fire the rocket to see if their design works (your physics department will know all about this). They are using mathematical skills such as measurement, scale, volume and circumference, as well as social skills such as team work and planning. There are endless cross-curricular opportunities between maths and science and the key is to make the time to liaise and talk to your colleagues in other fields.

Maths and geography

There are so many different ways in which mathematics links to geography, from population statistics, economics, scale and map reading to graphical representation. Liaise with the geography department; if they have an underlying theme for a series of lessons, then incorporate this into your mathematics. Linking with departments in this way also increases your exposure and ideas for the application of mathematics. You may have a plenary that has geographical application and starts to ensure pupils make connections. If you are completing a lesson on density then obtain some real-life statistical data from geography and ask pupils to calculate the population density of countries. Some of this may be comparative, such as calculating and comparing the population density in 1900 with the population density in 2000 (www.statistics.gov.uk has information on UK national statistics). You may borrow a set of atlases and ask pupils to estimate the distance between two cities given the scale. You may choose to start the lesson with a geographical problem, develop the mathematical theme during the lesson and then return to the problem in the plenary. Many different mathematical links can be built into the lesson and conversations with colleagues will reveal lots of different learning opportunities.

Maths and art

Art offers a fantastic window of opportunity for mathematics, from the wonderful patterns of symmetry, mosaics, transformations and 3D modelling to designing and making a kite. Mixing paint and observing the scale of colours from mixing different ratios is a powerful tool for visualising the impact of ratio and proportion and perhaps a nice simple way to start early. There are some wonderful ideas at http://nrich.maths.org.

Maths and social studies

There are some excellent resources as part of the Millennium Mathematics Project (see http://motivate.maths.org/content/MultiMediaResources). These include looking at the mathematical modelling of disease dynamics (epidemiology) and maths and our health or the impact of disease on public health.

The packages are multimedia and provide a good application of mathematics for pupils of school age to appreciate along with a useful source to promote interest. All are fields of research at the top universities throughout the world so offer wonderful insight into the world of mathematics beyond school.

Maths and physical education

There are lots of mathematical applications in PE and this is essentially to provide a flavour. Obvious cross-curricular links include averages such as the average time in which a pupil runs 100 metres, calculating the speed with which pupils run a given distance or track design (http://sport.maths.org has some nice ideas). One angle of PE that is interesting to explore for extension of mathematics is projectiles. Record pupils throwing a basketball and use the apps on the iPad to look at the trajectory fitting a parabola over the path. This offers real-life application to the mathematics of motion and an example is shown in *Mathematics: made to measure* (OFSTED 2012a).

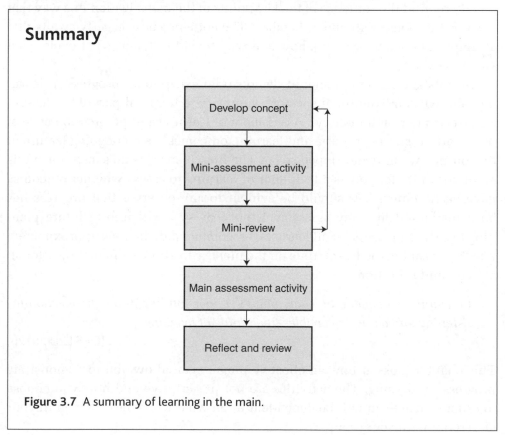

Summary

Figure 3.7 A summary of learning in the main.

CHAPTER 4

So how does it all end?

Let's return to the murder mystery analogy. The plot thickened; the inspector had a suspect and developed proof and understanding of how and why. He used different methods of investigation (some worked and some didn't), and applied different techniques to different suspects. There were mini case summaries along the way. He proved who did it and how, but can he succinctly remind the audience of the key points of the investigation in a way that ensures they can recall and remember? The audience now eagerly awaits that all-important summary: who, how and why they did it, and what we learned along the way.

An outstanding lesson should demonstrate exceptional progress in learning, and we can liken the inspector's summary to the final part of the lesson, (referred to here as a plenary). Assessment of learning and progression against personalised success criteria and learning outcomes are an ongoing feature of the journey we have developed so far. The final plenary is no exception and is an opportunity for you as a facilitator of learning to assess whether outcomes have been achieved. It should be evident to any observer that progress has been made and that any assessment made by you will inform future planning to secure progress for all learners. I recommend dedicating approximately 20–25 per cent of the lesson time on the plenary to allow sufficient time for an activity and reflection.

> *Constant assessment of each pupil's understanding through questioning, listening and observing enables fine tuning of teaching.*
>
> (OFSTED 2012b)

This chapter looks at how an effective plenary can allow you to demonstrate progress in learning. The activities are not prescriptive and how you choose to order or use them will be dependent upon what works best for you in your classroom with your groups.

Returning to the Big Question

Rather than asking pupils at the end of the lesson to indicate how well they had met learning objectives, some effective teachers set a problem which would confirm pupils' learning if solved correctly or pick up any remaining lack of understanding.

(OFSTED 2012a)

The Big Question is an excellent tool to demonstrate progress in learning. Remember that at the start of the lesson pupils have a few minutes to put their initial responses to a Big Question in an envelope and seal it (different types of question styles are discussed in Chapter 2). In the plenary we return to the Big Question to see if, following the development phase, pupils can now approach the question with a deeper understanding of the underlying mathematical concepts, thus demonstrating progress in their learning to you, a possible observer and most importantly to themselves.

The more probing the question, the longer you will give to pupils to retry it. It may be two minutes, it may be seven minutes. However long you choose, once they have had the opportunity to return to the question, ask them to open their envelope and compare the answer they gave at the start of the lesson to the answer at the end.

What have they learned during the lesson? How do they know? Can they identify key mathematical processes or concepts? Have they developed their mathematical reasoning? Can they now use appropriate mathematical language? Can they justify answers and use mathematical argument? It is important that pupils reflect on the differences between their initial response and their response after the learning process. Using a comparative activity such as this helps to embed learning, develop thinking skills and to clearly demonstrate development in learning during the lesson.

There are many ways in which the Big Question can be used. As with any activity, in many ways it is how you use it to drive learning rather than the activity itself. Time should be spent on discussion and questioning to ensure that key points are embedded. Do not be afraid to highlight and address any misconceptions at this stage. This is an equally important part of pupil development. Wrong answers allow pupils to explore how a misconception has arisen and by welcoming wrong answers pupils do not fear making mistakes (the classroom becomes a safe and open environment) and pupils will be confident to have a go at higher order questions as they realise the importance of how unravelling an error (if they make one) can help to develop and secure their understanding.

Pupils add value to an activity when they know that you value their input. It is therefore important to collect the envelopes in or ask pupils to stick initial and final responses in their books and ensure that you comment. Be prepared that the initial response may be blank or a question mark. That's okay as long as the pupil simply can't be bothered (if this is the case then don't be disheartened, they will soon want to be involved with the success they see others making). Entering into a teacher–pupil dialogue is the important part.

Extracts taken from actual pupil responses to Big Questions are given in Examples 4.1–4.5.

Example 4.1
A rectangle has sides 5 cm and 7 cm measured to the nearest centimetre. What is the area of the rectangle?

Initial response: 5 × 7 = 35
Final response: max width: 5.5 cm   max length: 7.5 cm   so   max area < 5.5 × 7.5 cm^2
Min width = 4.5 cm   min length = 6.5 cm   so   min area = 4.5 × 6.5 cm^2
So the area is anywhere between 29.25 and 41.25 cm^2 (it will be less than the latter value as otherwise lengths rounded up).

This promotes discussion about units (missing from the initial response) and about measurements and accuracy. Further points can be discussed to consolidate why the maximum area must be less than *41.25 cm^2* and how we can use mathematical notation to better represent the answer.

Example 4.2
A rectangle has sides (2*a* + 1) and (3*a* – 2). What is its area?

Initial response: 5*a* – 1
Final response: (2*a* + 1) × (3*a* – 2) = 2*a*(3*a* – 2) + 1(3*a* – 2) = 6*a*^{2} – 4*a* + 3*a* – 2 = 6*a*^{2} – *a* – 2
Initial response: (2*a* + 1) × (3*a* – 2) = 6*a* – 2
Final response: rectangle method (pupil had demonstrated this) to give 6*a*^{2} – 1*a* – 2

Again, these responses gave rise to the opportunity to discuss the different methods used, notation (e.g. *a* or 1*a*) and collection of like terms.

Example 4.3
Simplify the expression 3*a*^{5} × 2*a*^{10}

Initial response: 6*a*^{50}
Final response: 6*a*$^{(5+10)}$ = 6*a*^{15}

In discussing this pupils could be asked to reinforce quickly on mini-whiteboards why we add the powers, e.g. *a*^{2} × *a*^{3} = *a* × *a* × *a* × *a* × *a* = *a*^{5}. The skill here is ensuring that pupils understand the mathematical concept rather than just use a rule that they have learnt.

Example 4.4
Paul says, 'What's it worth?'

For this Big Question pupils were shown an image of a grid and had no information with which to answer the question, so only five seconds was allowed for an initial response (this adds a bit of fun to the lesson – someone may have guessed correctly!). The final response involved summarising their own working following a rich task relating to 'What's it worth?' (NRICH task: http://nrich.maths.org).

Example 4.5
Kate says, 'The probability that it will rain tomorrow is 50 per cent because it will either rain or not rain.'

Pupils are asked to agree or disagree with the statement. During the lesson the concept of probability is introduced and at the end of the lesson the statement is returned to briefly, with pupils asked to develop their mathematical reasoning and justify their answers.

The Big Question really helps to support success with pupils. Pupils feel a sense of achievement in being able to clearly demonstrate progress in their learning from the beginning of the lesson to the end.

Other ideas for the Big Question

There are lots of different ways that this comparative response activity can be used and the length of time dedicated really depends on how you choose to use or develop it. It may be a very simple assessment opportunity and take five minutes in total (leaving time for a further activity or reflection) or it may take ten minutes. Below are a few ideas:

- Differentiate the Big Question with different levels of challenge. These can be linked to your differentiated learning outcomes, levels and grades or success criteria.

- Use peer assessment and ask pupils to review a partner's initial and final response linked to assessment criteria.

- Use Post-it notes on a name board rather than envelopes so that pupils can stick their ideas on the board (particularly useful if you have a restless class). You can then select initial and final responses to discuss as a class or pupils can add to their answers at key points during the lesson as they develop mathematical concepts. This works well during investigative lessons.

- Use the activity as a team activity (large envelopes and sugar paper) and team review at the end of the lesson.
- Give different teams different Big Questions. Let them become the teacher. Give the rest of the class one minute to do the question and at the end of the lesson ask the team to present their initial and final responses to the rest of the class, who will judge the final response.

Plenary activities

If you choose to keep the Big Question short or not use it at all (after all you don't want to do the same every lesson and the very best teachers use a variety of different styles and types of activity) then you really need an outstanding plenary in its place. The plenary is an opportunity to demonstrate outstanding teaching and learning which does not have to involve 'all singing, all dancing activities', but does need to enable pupils to make connections between topics and to see the bigger picture. It should allow for metacognition and encourage mathematical independence, encouraging debate and discussion.

An outstanding plenary should enable you to judge the progress of **all** learners. Questions used during the plenary should not be more of the same. Outstanding plenaries use applied questions that offer further challenge and ensure that the pupils need to apply their knowledge and thinking skills and demonstrate a deeper understanding of the mathematical concepts rather than repeating a rote learnt method. For exam classes, applied exam questions or exam questions that involve combining mathematical skills and making connections are a secure choice. In order to achieve outstanding pupils need to:

- understand important mathematical concepts
- be able to make connections within mathematics
- be able to use and apply mathematics using a range of skills
- show exceptional independence
- take the initiative in solving problems in a wide range of contexts.

The plenary is an opportunity to reinforce this. I recommend getting a set of mini-whiteboards (laminated A4 card is a good alternative) as they allow you to assess the learning of the whole class. No pupil can escape being involved and therefore you are demonstrating assessment of your class individually and collectively. If your school has access to iPads or alternative tablet devices, then these are very effective for use in whole-class assessment. You can use them as mini-whiteboards and if you have an Apple TV connected to the whiteboard you can link instantly to any of the pupil's individual iPads to display their answer for the whole class from which you can deepen discussions.

When you pose the plenary question or problem always ensure that you allow pupils sufficient time to answer and then draw discussion from the answers that pupils have written. If you don't do this you are not demonstrating that pupils can justify their answers and the plenary will not be outstanding. It is your use of questioning that can make for an outstanding plenary. Use higher-order questioning (make sure it is hands down so that you target all learners) to probe pupils thinking. Remember, basketball questioning (develop questions from pupil to pupil as a team of learners) and not ping-pong questioning (teacher–pupil–teacher–pupil)! One last reminder is to ensure pupils can make reference to the level or grade of the question and have an understanding of what they need to do to ensure they get full marks in the exam (whether a GCSE or A-level or other public examination class).

Other plenary activity ideas

Correcting a response

Put the answer to a question on the board and ask pupils to comment on the answer. Pupils must identify any errors made, correct them and ensure that they use the correct mathematical reasoning. You can put emphasis on any aspect of mathematics. This can be a whole-class activity (using mini-whiteboards) or a paired or team activity. Alternatives include having the questions on A3 scattered around the room. Pupils can move around the room in teams (each team having a different coloured pen) and make comment on the answers. Time this activity to allow each team only 30 seconds or so on each question. When the round-robin is complete and each team has visited each question, you can stick the A3 paper on the board and use the questions as a discussion point. This type of activity can also be used with blank questions, where pupils go round in teams and put the answer on the paper, adding to the response (or correcting the response) given by previous teams (Examples 4.6–4.8).

Example 4.6
$7^4 \times 7^8 = 49^{12}$

This draws pupils into the discussion surrounding the base numbers, i.e. we do not multiply the base numbers. Pupils can be asked to demonstrate why, e.g.

$$7 \times 7 \times 7 \times 7 \times 7 \times 7 \times 7 \times 7 \times 7 \times 7 \times 7 \times 7$$

So how does it all end?

Example 4.7

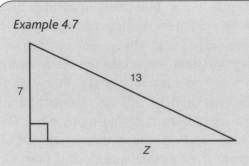

Figure 4.1 Find the length of side Z.

Answer 1
$Z^2 = 13^2 - 7^2 = 6^2$
Pupils need to identify that the numbers must be squared *before* they are subtracted.

Answer 2
$Z^2 = 13^2 - 7^2 = 169 - 49 = 120$
So $Z = 120$

The error here is that the pupil has not taken the square root of 120. Discussion here should be around thinking about whether answers actually make sense, i.e. 120 would be an extremely long side.

Example 4.8
Solve the inequality $8f + 1 < 25$

Answer
$8f < 24$ $f = 24/8$ $f = 3$

This is incorrect owing to the use of the equals sign, i.e. $f < 3$.

ABCD cards or collective voting mechanisms

These are very useful at KS3. Design a quiz (there are lots of templates on the internet, e.g. http://hotpot.uvic.ca, or design one yourself on PowerPoint) and ask pupils to hold up the correct response (A, B, C or D). The key to making this activity outstanding is the effective use of questioning. As a stand-alone activity, asking pupils to hold up an answer card is not outstanding; remember, like all activities, it is what you do with it! After each question target pupil responses, probe the learning and ensure it's not just a guess. Piggyback the questioning to develop the concepts further and pick up on any misconceptions should they arise. If you are lucky enough to have an interactive voting systems then this is an excellent way of recording pupil progress. Voting systems record responses by pupils to each question. You are then able to keep this information to support and inform future planning. The ABCD activity can be an individual, paired or team game (see Example 4.9).

Example 4.9
I invest £500 at 3 per cent per annum. What is the interest earned after three years?

A: £546.36

B: £45

C: £46.36

D: £545

In a situation where the majority of pupils hold up C, but some hold up A and B, you may choose to direct the questioning in a way that leads to picking up the misconceptions. For example:

'Paul, can you talk us through how you got C as an answer?'
'Karl can you develop this further?'

Piggyback questioning to other pupils.

'Amy, you chose B as your answer, can you talk through the method you used?'

Involve other pupils in the discussion. Encourage pupils to justify their answers rather than restate a method.

'Which is the method we use in the banking system?'
'What assumptions have we made?'

There are lots of ways in which this can be directed, but the point is that questioning is used to probe the answers. You may not wish to do this on every question but select a few where you feel the learning needs to be reinforced in order to secure the learning objectives. This is a rather closed example (having only one correct answer); of course, depending on the outcomes you wish to achieve, questions can be more open where the answer sparks debate between two responses.

Fun problems

These don't form a close to the lesson but are left open-ended to challenge pupils in their home learning. The plenary is effectively setting the scene, drawing from concepts developed during the lesson. There are some excellent ideas for these activities at the ATM website (www.atm.org.uk), NRICH maths (http://nrich.maths.org) or the STEM website (www.StemNet.org), or alternatively link with another subject and set a cross-curricular problem.

So how does it all end?

Making mathematical connections

Place an image on the board or around the room and ask pupils to spot the mathematics. This is quite a fun plenary and useful to reinforce mathematical links in everyday life or to support the cross-curricular nature of mathematics. At KS3 these can be simple images, such as a decorator with his tools about to paint a house after a lesson on proportion, the struggling chef who has a recipe for four when there are nine coming to a dinner party, best buy in supermarkets, financial investments, the pyramids for trigonometry or more complicated dynamic chemical simulations.

On the Futures Channel there are lots of short clips relating to real-life applications of mathematics (www.thefutureschannel.com). These can be used as a starter or a plenary. As a plenary play the clip and ask pupils to write down as many mathematical references and links that they can spot. Use the clip to then set the scene for home learning. Suffolkmaths has some good video clips (all of which have been reviewed by teachers). These can be found online at www.suffolkmaths.co.uk. ProblemPictures (www.problempictures. co.uk) brings maths to life with images and offers the teacher prompts for how to develop the underlying mathematics through questions.

Out of the hat

An activity popular at KS3, this is similar to pass the parcel. A hat (or container) is passed around the room and when the music stops the pupil with the hat has to pull out a question. This works well with key words and simple maths questions. Pupils may need to use the board to demonstrate an answer so, again, there is great variety in this activity. Aim to ensure that all pupils answer a question. As this activity involves the focus being on one pupil at a time rather than on the class as a whole (as with the other activities) then pace and classroom management are extremely important. If classroom management is a concern then a similar activity is a follow-me or loop card activity. These are where pupils have an answer and then a question on their card. You ask the first question. The pupil with the answer to this on their card identifies themselves and then reads out the question they have. This continues until all pupils have answered and asked a question. This type of activity will engage all learners because they need to listen carefully so that they do not break the chain.

Top Trumps

This activity is popular for younger years. Everyone is given a card, including the teacher. The cards are very similar to the cards that come with new toys. You can make your own, which enables you to tailor the cards to the learning needs. Once you have made them you can easily edit them for future use.

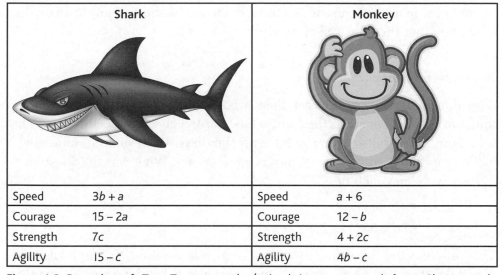

Shark		Monkey	
Speed	$3b + a$	Speed	$a + 6$
Courage	$15 - 2a$	Courage	$12 - b$
Strength	$7c$	Strength	$4 + 2c$
Agility	$15 - c$	Agility	$4b - c$

Figure 4.2 Examples of Top Trumps cards (animal images sourced from Shutterstock, www.shutterstock.com).

You can use this activity in lots of different ways:

- *Collectively*: You provide values for *a*, *b*, *c*, etc, and then ask pupils to identify whether they are faster or slower than the card you have. This can be made more challenging by using positive and negative numbers and asking pupils how, for example, the agility of their animal changes when we make *b* negative.
- *Different ability lines*: Give pupils four copies of their chosen animal. Around the room have four different lines, speed, courage, strength and agility. Ask pupils to place along the line where their animal should lie. Discussion can extend to which is the best animal overall.
- *A team game with groups of four*: Each team has the same cards and they have to decide who they would choose as the best character and why. Each team then presents their justification to the rest of the class and then the class have to debate as a whole as to which character they would choose and why, based on the arguments presented by each team.

So how does it all end?

You can make these cards quite easily in PowerPoint (which allows you to edit them for different games or skills). You can tie this activity in nicely with a Big Question at the start of the lesson: 'Pick the animal who is most courageous'. You can place images of lots of different animals on the board. Of course, pupils will be making a blind choice as they do not have enough information but at the end of the lesson they will be able to justify their response through the use of algebra. This just adds a bit of fun to the lesson and pupils really like to see whether they guessed correctly.

What was the question?

Give pupils the answer and ask them what the question was. Again, as you look around the room on the mini-whiteboards you can select answers that will form a good discussion point with the class. For example, following a 'collecting like terms' lesson, 'The answer is $2a + 1$. What was the question?'
    Answers may include:

$5a + 4 - 3a - 3$

$-5a - 4 + 7a + 5$

This provides the opportunity for discussion. For example, if a pupil has made a mistake then ask the class to try their suggestion for the question and then unpick the error.

Other suggestions include:

*   Anne and Claire ran each day this week. Each day Anne ran 3 miles in 30 minutes. Claire ran 6 miles in 72 minutes. The numerical answers are: 42, 2, 294, 3.5, 6

    What were the questions and what are the units? Have you made any assumptions?

*   Show two images with the second being a transformation of the first. Pupils are to write the question (choose an example that could have several possible transformations).

*   Two fractions are added. The answer is 5/8. What was the question? Again, a variety of different responses can be received, allowing discussion of fractions with different denominators, e.g. a simple response of (1/8 + 1/2) or (3/8 + 2/8) or (3/8 + 1/4) to (7/16 + 3/16)
    and so on.

*   A number rounded to one decimal place is 3.6. What was the number? This promotes discussion about the fact that numbers can range from 3.55

to 3.65. You often get most pupils limiting their answers to two decimal places, e.g. 3.61, so a good use of questioning and posing problems in the review can extend their thinking further and they can have a second attempt at the question, if necessary extending to, e.g. 3.5721 ...

Progression line

Set the learning outcomes out along a progression line and ask pupils to place a Post-it note (with their name on) next to the outcomes with a mathematical example of how they know they have met the outcome. Select these and use them for discussion. Asking pupils to offer an example removes the opportunity for pupils to say they have achieved an outcome without backing it up with the mathematics. A variation of this is to not set learning outcomes at the beginning of the lesson but ask pupils at the end to identify what they think the learning outcomes or objectives for the lesson were. This involves them thinking about the mathematical concepts that they have developed during the lesson.

For example, following a lesson on straight-line graphs (using all four quadrants) you place the following statements along a progression line (or ask pupils to place them in the order of difficulty):

- I understand the effects of a positive gradient and the coefficient of x, e.g. $y = 3x + 2$
- I can identify and interpret graphs with a positive coefficient and negative gradient, e.g. $-2x + 4$
- I understand the effects of a fractional gradient, e.g. $y = -\frac{1}{2} x - 10$
- I can identify the equation of any straight line.

If pupils have developed podcasts then play some of them now. Display them on the school website if possible and create a student-led maths learning zone.

There are multiple different activities out there. Remember that an activity may look fantastic and be 'all singing, all dancing', but if you don't use it in a way that demonstrates outstanding learning and progress then it will not be outstanding. It is as simple as that. A lesson does not have to have lots of 'whizzy' activities to be outstanding, what it does have to do is show clear development in mathematical progress. I cannot emphasise enough that you are the most important tool in making this happen. Your choice of activity and pace of activity to suit your learners, and your direction and use of questioning, will be the essential components.

Time for reflection

Finally, following any 'plenary activity' there should be an opportunity for reflection and the best lessons have a culture of reflective practice, both learner and teacher. Reflection should be built into the lesson at appropriate points and certainly towards the end of the lesson as part of the plenary.

As part of this process pupils need to be able to signpost their learning and be confident in identifying the next steps in achieving their goals. Simply being able to do something isn't enough. Pupils need to be encouraged to want to keep challenging themselves and their mathematical learning. Grades or levels help to support this process. Whether you return to differentiated learning outcomes or use assessing pupil progress (APP) grids, which are grids that simply contain the topic and the topic criteria at different levels or grades under a given mathematical category, encourage pupils to identify where they are in their own learning and where they need to go to achieve their next steps.

A note of caution: plenaries that simply ask pupils to write down 'what they have learnt today' or to traffic light what they have learnt can be very meaningless activities. They don't encourage pupils to think. Unless you can see evidence in front of you (i.e. use of mini-whiteboards), how do you know they are not simply saying they were 'green'? An observer will see through this so if you use traffic lighting or similar then use it in relation to an activity that you can assess as a whole.

> In plenary sessions at the end of lessons, teachers typically revisited the learning objectives, and asked pupils to assess their own understanding, often through 'thumbs', 'smiley faces' or traffic lights. However, such assessment was often superficial and may be unreliable.
>
> (OFSTED 2012a)

Asking pupils to reflect on their learning and to write something in their books really only has impact if it forms part of a teacher–learner dialogue, such that you read it and comment on it and they respond in turn to your comments (you then know they have read the comments you spent time writing). If pupils write things in their books and they are not reviewed by you then the process is devalued, pupils know you don't look at it and they end up just writing anything rather than really thinking about the content of what they are writing, which renders the exercise pointless. This doesn't need to take up significant amounts of your time. It may be something you choose to do at the end of a two-week series of lessons or at the end of a unit of study.

Until pupils become confident in this activity, use prompts to guide them, but remind them that they need to justify each statement they make. Ideas for prompts are given in Table 4.1.

Table 4.1 Ideas for prompts.

Prompt
I did … well, because I can …
I need to work on … because …
My learning targets are … so that I can …
How I managed to answer the Big Question …
I achieved grade/level … because I can …
My next steps in learning are … to achieve … because I want to be able to …

Reverse bell work

The aim of the bell work at the start of the lesson was simply to settle pupils until the large majority had arrived and you were ready to start your lesson. They were basic numeracy questions or mathematical images and time was not wasted reviewing them at the beginning of the lesson. They are returned to at the end. Put them back up and as pupils leave ask them for their answer.

Home learning

This seems an appropriate point to discuss home learning, which of course can be set at any point during the lesson or series of lessons. Some opt to set a challenge to extend the plenary as a home-learning activity, making the home learning more of an investigative style, which leads to natural differentiation through the open-ended answers. This can be something fun, such as designing a snakes and ladders game that uses algebra and substitution (the plenary can be used to demonstrate this). The start of the next lesson can be used to play the games in pairs and review and critique. It can equally be an extended cross-curricular or thematic project developed over an academic term.

Home learning can take many forms and does not have to be paper based and more of 'the same'. Some of the very best homework activities involve application and support connections in real-life scenarios. The school's learning platform provides an ideal base to set home learning and not just as an opportunity to set a task as a Word document (which can just as easily be printed off) and then submitted and collected online. Indeed, setting up an online quiz in the learning platform that allows you to instantly receive individual pupil's numerical scores (and individual question scores) in your mark-book (if the answers can be marked automatically) is a really useful tool. Of course, this can also be linked to the parent portal page which means parents have access to their child's performance. If internet access is a problem for some pupils then the quiz can be printed off and completed on paper. You can also set up interactive games that can be accessed by other schools so pupils compete against pupils in their own and in other schools. An example of this is 'Speed Sums' (discussed in detail in a blog at http://blog.frogtrade.com/2011/12/15/frog-connects-schools-around-the-world).

Learning platforms also allow you to set up discussion forums. These need to be carefully monitored and rules and expectations need to be set up beforehand to ensure the quality of response. You can rate pupil responses, which can again link to your mark-book. This does take some setting up, but the technician responsible for your learning platform should be trained in this or can receive help from the learning platform's support department direct. Once you set up activities like this it becomes easy to adapt them for other topics.

Other uses include creating glossaries. This can be done quite nicely in mathematics as a homework activity, as you can ask pupils to post questions or situations that result in a given answer (similar to 'What was the question?' discussed above) or you can simply ask pupils to provide examples. Remember, though, that this may be difficult with some mathematics where diagrams are needed, so think carefully about the scenario in which you use this facility. The different postings can be discussed collectively as a class during a lesson in which pupils can debate further.

MyMaths is, of course, a popular and useful tool for home learning (www.mymaths.co.uk). Tasks and activities can be set and it provides instant feedback to pupils and to the teacher, linking directly to a mark-book, which allows you to monitor and track pupil performance.

Many home-learning activities (particularly if project based) are cross-curricular. For example, you may combine with science where a project involves mathematical representation and interpretation of results. You may be responsible for marking and reviewing the mathematical content and the science staff for the science content. As discussed in Chapter 3, working together, as departments, not only supports pupil development but also supports numeracy across the curriculum and ensures a cohesive delivery.

Summary

For a challenging Big Question that forms the plenary activity (timings illustrative only, based on a one-hour lesson):

Big Question (seven minutes)
Reflection (five minutes)
Reverse bell work (one minute)

Where the Big Question was simple and only needs a quick response, progress needs to be demonstrated with a plenary activity:

Plenary activity (seven minutes)
Reflection (three minutes)
Big Question (two minutes)
Reverse bell work (one minute)

No Big Question at all:

Plenary activity (five minutes)
Reflection (three minutes)
Reverse bell work (one minute)

Remember

- Always have a plenary activity that involves *all* learners
- Use the activity well to demonstrate progress
- Draw the learning with probing questions (make sure you don't talk too much!)
- Build in time for reflection.

CHAPTER 5

What's in a question?

Who questions much, shall learn much and retain much.

(Francis Bacon)

You are the best resource in your classroom so use yourself wisely because you can really develop learning through the use of probing questions. Good questioning techniques can challenge and embed learning and can make a lesson outstanding. As a facilitator of learning, if you find you are talking or explaining a mathematical point then ask yourself 'Can I turn this into a question? Can I draw the learning by asking the pupils probing questions?'

This chapter is about developing your questioning skills as a teacher and about developing the questioning skills of pupils.

No hands up

Teachers ask between 300–400 questions a day.

(Levin and Long 1981)

The questioning technique you use and the quality of questions you ask is therefore extremely important. If you ask a question and then always ask the few who put their hands up, then you may find that some learners become the forgotten few or never answer a question. They can be the learners who disengage and don't actively participate or the leaner who is simply too quiet to offer an answer. Create a safe atmosphere. Ensure pupils are comfortable offering an answer whether it is correct or incorrect. Remember, wrong answers can often really help to develop learning because they pick up on misconceptions.

Always adopt a 'hands down' policy. This way learners have to keep on their toes, they have to listen to you and pay attention during the lesson because you could ask them next. In addition, ensure that in every lesson you have asked all pupils to respond to a question; this can be done skilfully by bouncing questions around the classroom in the same way a basketball team passes the ball among themselves (you are part of this team). Ping-pong questioning, in which the questioning is from you to pupil and back to you, doesn't always allow pupils to develop answers collectively and your input initially can be too high and too soon. When you ask pupils for responses ask a few pupils and then ask the class to decide on which answer offers the best explanation. This can be as simple as a statement such as 'Kate, do you have anything to add to that response?', or 'Pauline, what are your thoughts?', or 'Oliver, do you have a question to ask Kate?' (based on the previous answer).

Directing the questioning in this way allows you to differentiate. Questioning is an excellent tool for differentiation and will be further discussed in Chapter 7.

Wait and thinking time

Another important aspect of questioning is wait time and thinking time. Research shows that the average wait time for the response to a question is one second or less (Cotton 1988). This is far too short and often teachers jump on the first response, which doesn't allow pupils sufficient thinking time. Count to one and you will see! It puts pupils under far too much pressure and the quality of answers will be reduced. Try making a conscious effort to extend this thinking time to three seconds for lower-order cognitive questions and more than this (up to seven seconds) for higher-order cognitive questions. It may feel unnatural to have a silent pause, but remember that it allows pupils time to develop the answer in their own mind and hopefully improves the quality of response when this is shared with the class. This will also improve learner confidence. Higher-order cognitive questions require more wait time and increased wait time leads to higher-order cognitive discussions. Remember that you may give pupils longer if the question requires them to complete a short task before discussion takes place.

Wait time works both ways. Don't rush your response. Leave a short pause before you either bounce the question around the class or you respond to summarise. It allows you to recycle and gives other pupils in the class reaction time. Create cliff-hangers! This is a really powerful questioning technique. Getting this right can give your lesson that outstanding edge.

Responding to an incorrect answer

Believe it or not, incorrect answers are wonderful. Why? Because they allow you to really delve deep into pupil thinking and correct any misconceptions. If a pupil answers incorrectly, bounce the question around the classroom and see if pupils spot the misconception and encourage them to offer solutions as to how to correct it. Once you have probed the pupils and managed to secure the correct response or work towards the correct response you can offer your input (that is, a summary ensuring the correct technical language and method). Recapping in this way further secures the learning and you may ask pupils to pause and summarise the response to this question. This may lead to you asking a similar question a few minutes later to ensure that pupils have really corrected the misconception.

Open and closed questions

There are two types of question: closed and open. At its simplest level a closed question is one in which the answer is 'yes' or 'no' or requires a simple statement of fact and an open question is one that allows for discussion and openly encourages pupils to think. For example:

- Is 11 a prime number? (a closed question)
- Why is 11 a prime number? (an open question)

The closed question elicits a 'yes' or 'no' answer and does not probe pupils' understanding of prime numbers. The open question asks pupils to explain why 11 is a prime number and in doing this they must discuss the properties of number.

Or you may choose to bounce questioning around the room, starting with a closed question and progressing to open questions (Example 5.1).

Example 5.1
- 'Is 11 a prime number?'
- 'Why?'
- 'Give me another prime number that is less than 20.'
- 'So is 1 a prime number?'
- 'Can you explain your answer?'
- 'So can we now summarise the properties of a prime number?' (You will need to validate this response and at this point you ensure the correct technical language.)
- 'In pairs, circle the prime numbers on the number grid.' (Pupils are given a number grid with numbers 1 to 100.)

In this way you have developed the concept of prime numbers, resulting in a short activity to check their understanding. On completion of this activity (I suggest make it a race against the clock activity) you can regroup as a class and use questioning again to ensure that pupils have the correct numbers circled.

Start with one pupil and work around the class asking them to say the next prime number, explaining why it is a prime number. This embeds the learning through repetition. Pick up on any incorrect numbers and ask pupils to correct their own error by asking them the properties of a prime number and then asking them to further think as to whether the number they have suggested really is prime.

Bloom's taxonomy

You will have no doubt read or heard about 'Bloom'. Bloom's taxonomy (Bloom and Krathwohl 1956) classifies questions according to their level of cognitive demand. During the 1990s a new group of cognitive psychologists, led by Anderson (a former student of Bloom), updated the taxonomy to reflect relevance to 21st century work (Anderson and Krathwohl 2001: 67–68). The system contains six levels which are based on hierarchical form and which move from the lowest level of cognition (thinking) to the highest level of cognition of remembering, understanding, applying, analysing, evaluating and creating (this compares to Bloom's original taxonomy of knowledge, comprehension, application, analysis, synthesis and evaluation). Note that 'the top two levels are essentially exchanged from the old to the new version' (Schultz 2005). There is a movement from nouns to verbs, for example, application to applying. Let's look at each level and think about how this fits into questioning in mathematics.

Remembering

Remembering is the lowest level and simply involves the recall of facts. For example:

1) What is 3×4?
2) What is the formula for the area of a rectangle?
3) How many grams are in a kilogram?
4) What is the rule when we multiply numbers written in index form, e.g. $3^2 \times 3^4$?

- *Generic prompts include*: What did …? Who did …? How many …?
- *Words often used include*: know, who, define, what, name, where, list, when.

Understanding

Understanding is the way in which data are organised into categories or methods are used. For example:

1) What is the difference between a whole number and a percentage, for example 20 and 20 per cent? (This encourages pupils to compare and contrast categories of number.)

2) Find the gradient of the line. (This encourages pupils to recall and use a method.)

3) Why is 16 a square number?

4) Why are both −5 and 5 the square root of 25?

5) What is BODMAS?

6) What does the ratio 5:2 mean?

- *Generic prompts include*: Why did …? What are/does …? Why has …? Can you explain …?
- *Words often used include*: describe, use your own words to, outline, explain, discuss, compare.

Applying

Applying is where pupils take information they already know and apply it to different situations to reach a solution. Examples include:

1) Application of Pythagoras; for example, ladder against a wall problems as shown in Figure 5.1. A 12 foot ladder is resting against a wall such that the bottom of the ladder is 8 foot from the base of the wall. How far vertically up the wall does the ladder reach?

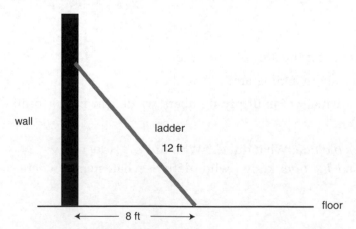

Figure 5.1 Application of Pythagoras.

2) Using formulas for area to find the area of compound shapes, for example, find the area of the shape in Figure 5.2.

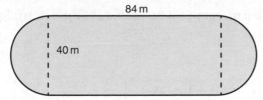

84 m

40 m

Figure 5.2 Compound area.

3) Best-buy questions, where pupils are asked to apply their knowledge and compare two deals. For example, a supermarket is offering three for two on its products. A small bag of 80 teabags costs £1.40 and a large bag of 320 teabags costs £3.70. Milo wants to buy 320 teabags. Which is the better deal?

4) Find 31 per cent of 72.

5) How do you round a number to the nearest 100?

6) Simplify the ratio 32:40.

7) What are the next three numbers in the sequence 2, 5, 8, 11, … and how do you find a general rule for the nth term?

- *Generic prompts include*: How can you …? How would you …? Using this information can you …?
- *Words often used include*: apply, demonstrate, calculate, illustrate, classify, discover, solve, compare.

Analysing

Analysing involves pupils breaking down a problem and looking at it in different ways. Pupils need to provide reasons and reach conclusions. The problems require pupils to spot a pattern and identify key parts of the question. Examples include:

1) Encourage pupils to analyse different methods of data collection and select different scenarios that each would be appropriate to.

2) Give pupils two different graphs that offer similar information, for example, boys' and girls' heights in a box plot. Ask pupils to analyse the information and come to conclusions.

3) Which is the square number closest to 40?

4) Explain why if we increase 300 by 25 per cent we add the same amount as we take off if we decrease the result by 20 per cent.

5) If $x = 5$ and $y = 3$ which of these is bigger and by how much: $3x^2$ or $y^3 + 5x$?

6) Is 250 a number in the sequence 3, 8, 13, 18, … ?

7) Can you identify which is the incorrect point in Table 5.1 to plot a straight-line graph? Explain your answer.

Table 5.1 Data for a straight-line graph.

x	2	5	10	15
y	5	11	25	31

8) What happens when we change the gradient of the line for the equation $y = 3x + 2$ to $y = -3x + 2$?

- *Generic prompts include*: What are …? Why did …? Why do …? What if …? Consider …? Discuss …

- *Words used include*: analyse, connect, arrange, compare, select, explain, infer, order.

Evaluating

Evaluating is where pupils make connections between different areas of mathematics, engage in creative thinking and stand by and justify decisions. These questions cover a range of possible responses. It involves pupils relating mathematics from different areas and reaching conclusions. Examples include:

1) How would you find the percentage discount in this clothing advert given what we have learnt today?

2) Which number up to 100 has the most factors?

3) Can you use the line of best fit you have drawn on the scatter graph to predict the height of a pupil with shoe size 6? Are everybody's results the same?

4) How do you show that fractions are equivalent?

5) Which is bigger, 16 per cent of 35 or 3/20 of 35?

6) List two fractions that lie between 1/3 and 1/2.

7) How do you check that your factorising is correct?

- *Generic prompts include*: How would you …? Construct a … Are everybody's results the same …?

- *Words used include*: prepare, generalise, create, plan, substitute, modify.

Creating

Creating is where pupils create a new rule or generalisation. To accomplish creating tasks, learners generate, plan and produce. Examples include:

1) Find the equation of two lines passing through the point (3,8).
2) Design a reflection that is difficult. What makes it difficult?
3) Can you write three expressions that would simplify to $2(3x + 1)$? How do you know? Are there more?
4) Create two different sequences where the fourth term is 20 and write down the general rule for both of them.
5) The answer is 3.2. What was the question?
6) A number is rounded to one decimal place to give 5.4. What was the number?

- *Generic prompts include*: What would have happened if …? Pretend that … Design a … Think of another way to …
- *Words used include*: assess, design, create, develop.

Summary

Research shows that 'approximately 60 per cent of the questions asked are lower cognitive questions, 20 per cent are higher cognitive questions, and 20 per cent are procedural' (Cotton 1988: 6). This is a particularly worrying fact as it implies that the majority of teacher questioning is in the lower-order cognitive bracket. In order to use questioning effectively in the classroom as a tool to promote learning there needs to be a shift to an increase in higher-order cognitive questioning, so really think about the quality of questions that you ask. Since many questions are created off the back of pupil responses, the questioning theme can be pre-planned but the 'bounced' questions cannot. This is why teacher response time is very important. Take the opportunity to pause and think carefully about how you are going to create a higher-order question to bounce back to pupils.

Think, pair, share

'Think, pair, share' is a cognitive rehearsal strategy and allows pupils to develop their answers before they are shared collectively as a class. Essentially you pose a question, allow pupils a short period of time to think individually about the question (perhaps 30 seconds), then they form a pair to discuss and develop their responses (one minute or so) and then this is shared as a class where it is discussed and further developed.

Probing questions to develop a concept

Probing questions in mathematics are important in developing mathematical concepts. In this section we look at specific mathematical topics and how we can probe learning through the questions we pose. The ideas developed here can then be applied to creating probing questions in other topics.

Finding the outcomes of percentage increase and decrease

For example, the owner of a clothes shop decides to put her prices up by 15 per cent. A jumper currently costs £40. What will it cost after the increase?

Pupils working through this are initially most likely to calculate 10 per cent (£4) and then 5 per cent (£2) and then add to the original to give £40 + £4 + £2 = £46. This is good because allowing pupils to do this provides a comparative method from which to build. Other pupils may work through the equivalence of decimals and percentages and find first 0.15 × £40 = £6 and then add this to the original to give £46.

You may then ask pupils, 'what about if goods had been increased by 20.14 per cent?' (they will then have to think a little deeper about their process).

Pupils can then be encouraged to think about diagrammatic representation. You can ask them how much in percentage terms the original is worth. They will need to think carefully and equate this to 100 per cent. You can then ask them what the 'new' amount is worth in percentage terms. Again they will need to think about '100 per cent plus 15 per cent is equal to 115 per cent'. Encourage pupils to complete the diagrammatic representation shown in Figure 5.3.

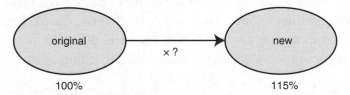

Figure 5.3 Diagrammatic representation for percentage change.

Ask pupils to think about what we multiply 100 by to get 115: 100 × ? = 115.

Ask pupils if they can find the relationship between the new percentage, original and the multiplier, i.e. 115/100 = 1.15.

Now ask pupils to use only the flow diagram with the original amount to get the new amount. Pupils will then try £40 × 1.15 = £46.

Ask pupils to investigate the reverse: if we were given £46 and asked to find the original how might they do this using the diagram? Discuss the relationship with division. Pose a further question with more difficult values and ask pupils to create a diagram and then discuss with their peers, e.g. house prices from 2001 to 2005 increased by 24 per cent. In 2005 a house cost £180,000. What would it have cost in 2001? Using the think, pair, share method here will promote discussion.

Having done this you pose a question based on percentage decrease, e.g. a car originally cost £12,000. Five years later it was valued at 12 per cent less. Can you find the price five years later? (Again encourage the use of the diagram to support thinking.) Ask pupils to discuss whether their answers make sense in magnitude and in line with the question.

This leads to the discussion of the 'new price' being worth 88 per cent of the original, leading to a multiplier of 0.88. Use questioning to probe this learning.

Pose a further open-ended question to allow a think, pair, share opportunity.

Once these methods have been established you may assess the learning with a series of questions and then a mini-plenary. Following this, introduce questions that ask pupils to find the percentage by which amounts have been increased or decreased. For example: a coat cost £125 in November. In the January sales it is priced at £80. What is the percentage reduction?

Promote the use of the diagram shown in Figure 5.4.

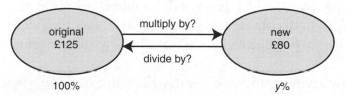

Figure 5.4 Percentage change.

Pupils may approach this by thinking about 125 × ? = £80 or alternatively 80/125 = ?

As pupils determine the value of '?' (0.64) the interesting discussions begin.

You will probably get a mixture of responses to the original question: 64 per cent or 36 per cent. This is where you need to encourage pupils to debate their responses actively. The correct answer is, of course, a reduction of 36 per cent, i.e. the 'new price' is worth 64 per cent of the original, which means it was reduced by 36 per cent.

There are lots of different ways you may choose to develop percentage increase and decrease, but by beginning to introduce diagrams you support the visualisation of mathematics and this can be used to make connections with other topics and to homogenise the method.

What's in a question?

Developing percentage increase in this way avoids the rote learning of methods and allows pupils to think about the information given in the question. Making connections through diagrammatic representation allows ideas to be embedded effectively. In other words, pupils are allowing the mathematics to flow and are not learning a separate method for percentage increase, percentage decrease, finding the percentage increase, finding the percentage decrease and finding the original, but one diagram that supports the underlying concept.

Trial and improvement

Pose the problem: $x^2 + x + 1 = 17$

Ask pupils what the value of x is. Pupils will work desperately on their calculators to try to find the value for x and you will most likely have 30 different answers. Ask pupils 'how they arrived at these answers'. The underlying technique being trial and error!

Develop this further and ask pupils which two integer values x lies between. Hopefully pupils will offer 3 and 4.

Now ask pupils to find the value of $x^2 + x + 1$ when $x = 3$ and when $x = 4$.

Ask them to determine whether the value of x is too small (i.e. the answer is less than 17) or x is too big (i.e. the answer is greater than 17).

Ask pupils to suggest a value they try next for x. Discuss whether it matters which value you choose between 3 and 4. Is one value a more sensible choice than another? Allow pupils to decide on this value and then continue until they determine two numbers to one decimal place that x lie between, for example, 3.5 and 3.6.

Then ask pupils to draw a number line and develop through questioning the concept of rounding illustrated in Figure 5.5.

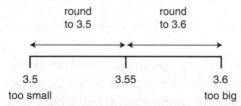

Figure 5.5 The concept of rounding to one decimal place.

Pupils are then asked which number they need to try next to determine the value of x to one decimal place (d.p.). Pupils then try 3.55. As they do this they determine that a value of 3.55 means x is too big (giving a value of 17.15) and therefore x must lie in between 3.5 and 3.55, meaning that to one decimal place $x = 3.5$ (1 d.p.).

Careful questioning here formalises the original trial-and-error method used by pupils initially and connects to the lower-level concept of rounding.

Enlargements

Construct an enlargement of a 2D shape. Ask pupils to:

- identify what changes and what stays the same
- use this information to find the *scale factor* for the enlargement
- investigate what effect a scale factor less than one has
- investigate what happens to the area of the shape.

Now give pupils a 2D shape on a coordinate grid that involves using a centre of enlargement. Give them two identical shapes, enlarged by the same scale factor (for example, two) but with different centres of enlargement. Ask them:

- to identify what is the same
- to identify what is different.

If pupils don't offer enlargement about a different point then point them in the right direction and provide them with a clue. Ask them how they can determine or find the point from which the shape is enlarged such that the distance from the point to the image is double (assuming a scale factor of two) that of the distance from the point to the object. Use this to develop enlargement with a scale factor given a centre of enlargement.

Note that this is very different from simply teaching pupils how to do an enlargement. Using this or similar techniques encourages pupils to think for themselves.

Standard form

Tell pupils 'The following numbers are written in what is known as standard form. What do you notice?'

$823 = 8.23 \times 10^2$
$5273 = 5.273 \times 10^3$
$52 = 5.2 \times 10^1$
$0.00643 = 6.43 \times 10^{-3}$
$0.43 = 4.3 \times 10^{-1}$

This will encourage pupils to note that each number is written as a number between 1 and 10 multiplied by a power of 10. You can then ask pupils to use this information to write a series of numbers in standard form. Ask them when standard form might be a useful form of notation, i.e. for very large or small numbers (e.g. link with science and diameter of planets, etc.). This can lead to problems using standard form. Note again that we are developing pupils' thinking skills through questioning and not simply stating the rules of standard form.

The addition of a constant or multiplication by a constant on a graph

This can be done using ICT (this is the best tool to use) or plotting by hand. The outcome isn't whether pupils can plot a graph but whether they can investigate the effects of a constant.

You may start with a pre-drawn graph of $y = x^2$. Task pupils in teams with investigating the effects of $y = x^2 + b$. Ask teams to predict first what they think will happen and then ask them each to choose different values of b (within a given range of your pre-drawn axes) and plot the graph. In their teams they are to put into words the underlying mathematics. Hopefully they will determine vertical translation parallel to the y-axis by the amount b. When the whole class return ask them whether they can explain why this is the case. Further, ask them what impact $b = -20$ will have on the graph. Does the shape of the graph change?

Continue this theme with the investigation of $y = ax^2$. Repeat the task above and then ask pupils to discuss their findings collectively. This can lead to asking pupils to predict/sketch the graph $y = 2x^2 + 3$. You can then ask them whether they can develop in their teams a video, podcast, blog or poster on how to do this (task each team with a different activity). Ask pupils what impact a value of 'a' less than 1 would have.

Finding an expression for the nth term

Ask pupils to write down anything they notice about the sequence 3, 5, 7, 9, 11, ...

Most pupils will spot the term-to-term relationship of 'add two' or 'going up in twos'. Ask pupils which other sequence of numbers they know that goes up in twos. Discuss the two-times table. Encourage pupils to write out the two-times table. Do they notice a link between the two-times table and the number sequence? Develop the ideas of 'add one'. In other words encourage pupils to say in words 'take the two-times table and add one'. Discuss how you could write that more mathematically, i.e. $2 \times n + 1$ or $2n + 1$. You can further develop questioning to embed this theme.

Teacher input

The aim of questioning is to allow pupils time to think for themselves and to make sense of mathematical concepts and naturally make connections between their ideas.

There are key points when a teacher or facilitator needs to intervene:

- When pupils need specific mathematical notation or words. For example, 'hypotenuse'; pupils in their development and investigation of Pythagoras refer to this as the longest side. Hypotenuse is a definition that pupils cannot pre-know.

- During consolidation a teacher may pull methods and ideas together, then offer alternative methods and ask pupils for their input in doing this. A teacher may also pull ideas from pupils together and reinforce the method or highlight mathematical concepts or ideas in their solutions. This can be done explicitly by probing with questions and drawing pupils' attention to these ideas.

- When pupils need guidance. This can be when the lesson is pulled back together and ideas are shared and any misconceptions are then highlighted. Once this is done questioning can direct pupils to a more productive line of enquiry.

Summary

Questioning is one of your most powerful tools as a facilitator of learning and one that you can work to develop. Ask a colleague (it can be cross-curricular) if you can observe their lesson. Focus on nothing but questioning. Note:

- how often they tell pupils something (keep in mind how you might have turned this into a question to draw learning from pupils)
- how often they ask questions and how often pupils ask questions of them (do a tally)
- how many of these questions are open or closed
- the cognitive level of the questions (are they lower or higher order)
- whether they adopt a hands-down policy
- who they ask – draw a rough plan of the room and each time a pupil answers a question or is asked a question put a cross; this will allow you to see the distribution of questioning (i.e. whether they always ask the same few, whether the same pupils offer solutions, whether they ask all pupils at some point during the lesson).

Once you have completed the observation think about how you would have changed things. Discuss this with your colleague and develop your questioning together. Ask your colleague to observe you with the focus being solely on questioning or, even better, video your lesson (ensure this is allowed within your school policy). This is a very powerful tool. You can watch the lesson back with someone and really note questioning behaviours, patterns and pupil responses. The next phase is to try to conduct a lesson in which you only ask questions and draw the learning through questioning; that is, you don't tell pupils anything. Video this lesson and focus on the behaviours of the learners. If you don't have a high level of independent learning in your classroom pupils will struggle with this; that is, if you normally teach and they do. Persevere because the outcome is ultimately worth it. Next is to try to ensure a fine balance between your facilitation of learning with questioning and your input. This is where you will develop outstanding learning in your classroom.

So, in summary:

- when you plan your lesson think about the open questions you may want to ask
- think about using the vocabulary associated with higher-order thinking skills
- if you are about to 'tell pupils something' then stop and rephrase the statement as a question to develop their thinking skills
- encourage pupils to ask questions of you and each other
- promote a safe learning environment in which mistakes are welcomed as part of the learning process.

Remember:

It is not that I'm so smart. But I stay with the questions much longer.

(Albert Einstein)

CHAPTER 6

How do I know?

Assessment is something that, as teachers, we do all of the time, explicitly or not. When we observe the class, we are making an assessment. When we listen to the answer to a question, we are making an assessment. When we circulate and talk to individuals, we are making an assessment. The outcomes of these assessments shape our 'teacher responses' in lessons. We may redirect learning or we may simply get affirmation that pupils have a good level of understanding and continue. Outstanding teachers use assessment as a powerful tool to drive learning and to check pupil progress.

It is important to be aware of the different types of assessment: assessment *for* learning, assessment *as* learning and assessment *of* learning.

Assessment *for* learning is formative assessment. It is ongoing, diagnostic and involves the dialogue for assessment between pupil and teacher (verbal or written feedback). Generally it happens during the learning process and is interactive. Teachers differentiate and create learning opportunities for individuals based on assessment for learning. Assessment for learning was strongly advocated by Wiliam and Black (1998) and is now very much at the heart of school improvement strategies.

Assessment *as* learning involves pupils assessing their own learning and involves self-assessment and peer assessment. It is an ongoing process. It develops pupil's involvement in their own learning. Pupils develop their metacognitive skills.

Assessment *of* learning is a summative process. It involves mainly teacher assessment and results, for example, in a grade or some form of attainment measure. It is the most commonly sought feedback from pupils: 'Which grade am I?'

Against what?

Assessment is powerful but only as powerful as the quality of criteria against which the pupils are being assessed or measured.

How robust are your learning outcomes? How accurate are the grades linked to the respective outcomes? Have you accurately moderated summative assessments? How did you arrive at the target grades for pupils? Are the target grades fluid or fixed? What do you do with information obtained from assessments? Are pupils involved in assessment of their own learning? Do pupils read what you write when you assess work or is it just something you do in line with school policy?

All of these questions need to be addressed. For anything to be successful and play an integral role in learning it has to be valued by the teacher, pupil and parent.

Learning outcomes and success criteria

Learning outcomes are an essential part of the learning process. They summarise the purpose of the lesson. Success criteria further dissect the outcomes to a series of achievable 'chunks'. Success criteria support pupils in assessing their own progress towards meeting the learning outcomes. Essentially, they become a checklist (but be careful they don't tell pupils how to do something; ensure that you don't issue success criteria with too much information if you choose to give them out at the start of the lesson!).

Consider the simple learning outcomes: *I will*

- develop a method for expanding two linear brackets, e.g. $(2x + 1)(3x - 5)$
- be able to apply this to solving problems in different contexts.

Success criteria (i.e. a tick list that pupils can return to during the lesson as they achieve each criterion. These can be referenced links to specific activities in the lesson as appropriate).

- I can expand a single term over a bracket, e.g. $2(3x + 4)$
- I can expand two simple linear expressions, e.g. $(x + 2)(x + 5)$
- I can expand liner expressions where the coefficient of x is not 1, e.g. $(3x - 4)(2x + 1)$
- I can apply the expansion of two brackets to area problems and problems where a diagram is given (give reference to questions which require this skill on the learning resource you are using)
- I can select the appropriate method from problems that are word problems only, i.e. I can interpret and relay the information as a diagrammatic representation and then use expanding brackets to solve the problem (give reference to questions that require this skill on the learning resource you are using)
- I can combine expanding brackets with other mathematical concepts in context (give reference to questions that require this skill on the learning resource you are using).

You can attach a grade to each success criterion if you choose to do so. In doing this the success criteria become more of a progression ladder. In each lesson you should clearly identify the essential success criteria (e.g. in the list above these may be the first three criteria) that are necessary to achieve the learning outcomes, any additional criteria support extension.

Learning outcomes: I am able to find the area of 2D shapes

Success criteria:

- I can find the area of a rectangle, a triangle and a parallelogram
- I can identify the correct lengths to use, e.g. the vertical height of the triangle
- I can use the correct units of measurement for length and area
- I can find the area of simple compound shapes (involving the addition of two areas)
- I can find the area of shapes with 'missing pieces' (involving subtraction of areas).

Learning outcome: I will develop the rules for multiplying indices, e.g. $3^2 \times 3^5$

Success criteria:

- I can expand number written in index form, e.g. $3^4 = 3 \times 3 \times 3 \times 3$
- I can use this to help me find a general rule for multiplying two numbers in index form
- I can extend this to division
- I can use this to understand the meaning of negative indices.

Learning outcome: I will understand and be able to enlarge a simple 2D shape given a centre of enlargement and a positive integer scale factor

Success criteria:

- I can enlarge a simple 2D shape with a scale factor (no grid)
- I can enlarge a 2D shape given a scale factor and centre of enlargement (with grid)
- I understand the effect of a scale factor *0 < SF < 1*
- I understand the effect of a negative scale factor.

In the final example the first two points address the learning objective and the last two can be for extension purposes. Success criteria allow for differentiation. You can colour code them as to those essential in achieving the learning outcomes and those that extend the learning outcomes further.

Quality interaction with pupils

How you interact with pupils is important. Here we discuss not whole-class interaction (covered previously), but interaction with pupils during the learning phase. This is when pupils are completing an activity. For example, pupils may be working individually on a series of questions or pupils may be involved in a group activity. Circulating around the class and ensuring that you observe all pupils is important. You know the weaker pupils in your classroom and these should be the ones that you target first. Ensure they are confident with the activity. Probe their thinking with questions or add helpful prompts. Offer encouragement and praise and if you spot an error pick up on it quickly. The dialogue you have with pupils during this phase may be more fruitful than the whole-class discussions. This is simply because some pupils will be more cautious when discussions are in front of their peers as a class.

As you go around note carefully any points that would be interesting to discuss when you pull the class back together. If pupils are working in groups, then this can be an opportunity for you to sit and observe or assess. Join the group and add to their discussions. Listen, ask questions and make them think. The questions don't have to be answered there and then.

When you pull the class together to review the activity ask individuals by name to discuss certain issues. This may be a pupil who had made an error and you would like them to come to the board to discuss what they did wrong and how they corrected it. You can then invite contributions from others. It may be that a pupil has managed to complete an interesting application question and you would like them to share it with the rest of the class. You may have pulled the class together because you have noticed that several of them are making the same error. This allows you to probe pupil thinking before continuing with the activity.

Whole-class interaction is done mainly through observation and questioning. Observing a task or activity when pupils are all completing it individually or in pairs is a form of assessment. Whole-class questioning (discussed in Chapter 5) is the most common form of interaction with the entire class: questioning to develop a concept and questioning to probe understanding.

Target setting

This is a much-debated area in education; however, whether you agree with targets or not they are very much a part of our education system. I don't personally believe in setting single target grades for pupils based on their attainment in a 'test' at a given age that is then used to support (along with other factors such as socioeconomics) estimates on performance in future examinations. Should we really be giving pupils a ceiling? Should we not want them to aim high? Imagine being the pupil with a target grade of E in mathematics. The moment you are issued with that target you are labelled and feel like, a failure (before you've even started the course of lessons). You feel like you are never going to achieve the baseline C grade needed for college or further education. So how do you behave in mathematics lessons? Do you engage with the learning? Do you put more effort into other subjects where there is hope that you will pass? Of course, each pupil is an individual and will react differently. However, I encourage you to think carefully about this when setting pupils target grades: don't demotivate from the outset.

Much more beneficial is the use of grade distributions. The most likely grade (based on prior performance) may be a grade D, for example, but from the grade distribution there is a possibility of a grade E, C or B (or even higher, although probabilities will be far smaller here). Share this with pupils. Make their target a grade spectrum from D to B. Explain to them that while their most likely grade may be a D, if they work really hard they could get a B (or if they don't put effort in a grade lower than D). This doesn't label pupils as a failure from the outset but now gives them aspiration.

How do you then monitor performance if you use a range of grades as a target? I agree that performance and management systems require a single grade to measure relative performance. Therefore use the most likely grade in your data-management systems to which you can then compare performance. For example, a pupil who has a most likely grade of D (but a grade distribution of E to B) performs to a C in an examination. They would then be highlighted (perhaps green in a colour-coded system) as performing a full grade above their most likely grade (indicated, perhaps, as +1). Your data management system can then be used to monitor performance from one data input to the next, noting improvement.

You could use $-2, -1, 0, +1, +2$ to indicate performance relative to the most likely grade (two grades below, one grade below, etc.) and then colour code according to performance relative to the previous data input. An example is shown in Table 6.1.

Table 6.1 An example of a tracking grid (AP, assessment point).

	Target grade	AP 1	AP 2	AP 3
Pupil 1	D	1	1	0
Pupil 2	B	0	−1	1
Pupil 3	A	0	0	−1

In this table we can see that while Pupil 1 is on target at assessment point 3 (AP3), i.e. an indicator of 0, they have actually underperformed relative to the previous assessment. I would therefore colour this cell red to highlight a decline in progress from the previous assessment point. This then immediately draws my attention to the fact that there has been a drop in progress despite the pupil performing at their 'most likely grade' (a numerical indicator of 0). The colour coding allows for tracking by progression (red, underperformed relative to previous assessment; blue, remained the same as previous assessment; green, improved on the previous assessment) and the numerical entry allows a summative performance relative to the target grade (–1, one grade below target; 0, on target; 1, one grade above target, etc.). This system of tracking therefore provides two types of assessment. Ideally we would want to see cells with numerical values greater than or equal to 0 that are colour coded blue (to indicate consistent performance) or green to demonstrate improvement.

Target grades are only estimates and should therefore be reviewed at key points. They shouldn't be fixed and remain set in stone for the duration. They are formed based on statistical data for similar cohorts based on prior attainment, and we all know that there are exceptions to the rule and that many pupils can suddenly just 'make the connection' and 'get it'. My advice is to use them along with the many other factors and pieces of information that are available to you as a professional. One final note: have you discussed what target grades really mean with each pupil? Have they been involved in the process and do they understand the process? Or is it simply a grade on a page, there to be referenced if someone asks? Do their parents or guardians understand what a target grade means? Communication to avoid miscommunication is vital.

The quality of assessments

Any tracking system is only as good as the quality of data that it uses. If the assessments you use are not accurately moderated then the information obtained from them will be meaningless. In moderating assessments both the writing of and the marking of are important. There can be great in-house variation in the quality of marking and so it is important to moderate this to ensure consistency across a year group. This is the only way that you are able to make comparisons across groups.

The quality of the assessment is critical. Assessments must be accurately moderated; if you are grading assessment papers as A, B, C, …, then do these grade boundaries accurately equate to the external national assessment grading? In other words, if a pupil continually achieves a grade C in in-house assessments is that suggestive of performance at a grade C in external examinations?

Moderate as a department and, if necessary, invite experts in to support this process. There are lots of resources out there, such as exam banks which offer graded material. In addition, for example, past graduated or modular assessment examinations offer graded questions (e.g. OCR Stage 7 containing grade C GCSE questions). However you choose to assess, ensuring the quality of outcome is paramount.

A further point for thought is whether the assessments you use allow for a range of learning styles. For example, are all of your assessments written? Do you assess activities, such as podcasts or video links? Try to allow assessment points to cover a range of learning styles.

Marking and feedback

How often do you mark pupils work? How confident are you that the pupils read what you have written or review any comments you have made? Do you feel pressured to mark every piece of work in a pupil's book? Has marking simply become a habit because of a whole-school marking policy, often written by those who rarely teach (and therefore have no books to mark!)? Is your marking worthwhile?

We must not forget that marking commands a significant amount of a teacher's time. Let's be blunt: it is a waste of time if it doesn't have any impact on the pupil learning process. In this section we look at how by marking less you can have a greater impact, quality marking over quantity. Consider a few key points discussed below.

Should work be graded?

This is a topic that is greatly debated. Caution needs to be taken when grading individual pieces of work. I say this because consider, for example, simplifying surds (at grade A). If a pupil gets most of the work incorrect does this make them a grade B? No it does not. Therefore grading individual pieces of work should air caution. Grading is there as a guide because mathematical learning is hierarchical and grading is a general indicator over a range of topics as a measure of mathematical ability or as an indicator of progression in certain topics. Research suggests that pupils do not benefit from grades and marks on their work (Black *et al.* 2003), and that when grades and comments are given the positive effects of the comment are detracted by the grade.

Perhaps better is that pupils are given an indication of whether the work is on target, above target or below target (with reference to meeting the learning outcomes T+, T, T−). This removes the issue of grading and supports marking for progress. Subject-specific targets can then be issued to pupils.

What do you write?

Marking with a 'well done, grade B' has little impact. I fully support the use of praise as I think that this supports the positive pupil–teacher relations (and pupils like to receive praise). However, it really has no impact on pupil progress. Better is to add a meaningful comment.

Some examples are given in Figures 6.1–6.3.

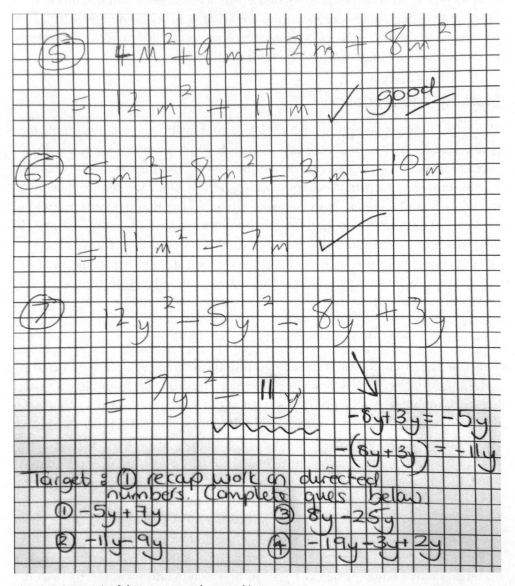

Figure 6.1 Meaningful comments when marking.

Comments should support pupil progress. There should also be dialogue between teacher and pupil. Pupils should be encouraged to read the comments and reply to them, acknowledging that they have read them and being free to reply to the comments.

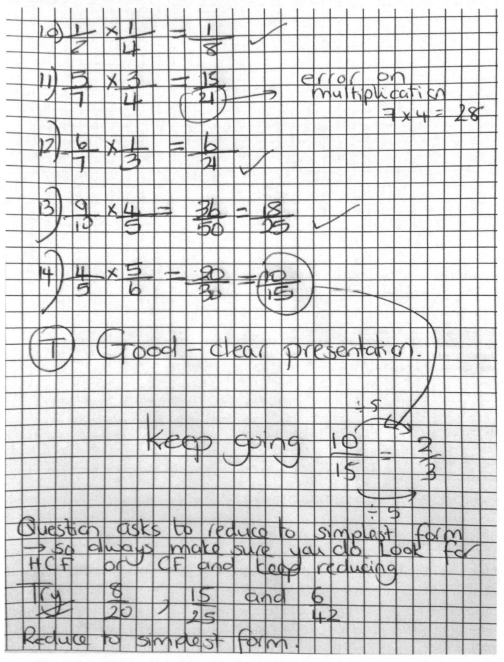

Figure 6.2 Meaningful comments when marking.

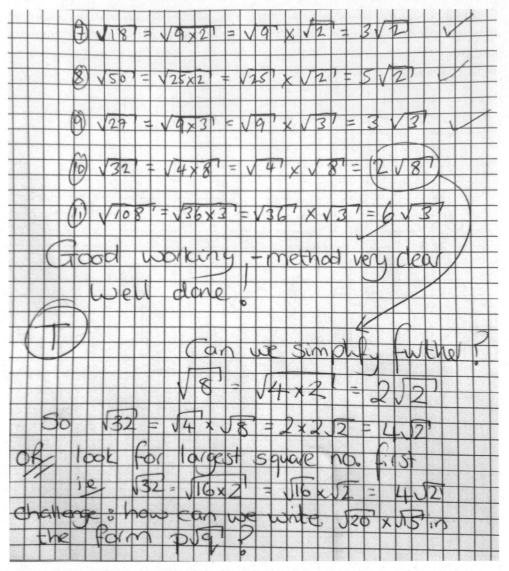

Figure 6.3 Meaningful comments when marking.

Active marking

One very useful technique in addition to this is to use Post-it notes. I add a Post-it note to each pupil's book as necessary when I mark at the end of a unit of work or topic, using different colours for different reasons. I use yellow Post-it notes when a pupil has made lots of errors and I set them a challenge to work on. I use pink Post-it notes if I feel that a pupil has grasped the general concepts but I need further confirmation on their understanding, so I set them a problem to work on that will confirm this. I use green Post-it notes for those pupils who have got everything correct and I want to set a task (in addition to those set in class) that will challenge their thinking further. Pupils have to write their response back on the Post-it note (or on a blank Post-it). I then take the Post-it notes in and review them. Pupils need to have read the comments about their work (written in their books) and reviewed their own work in order to respond to the Post-it. I have a simple A4 folder with a page for each pupil in the class. I then stick the Post-it note onto their page and place it in the folder. I often give pupils two minutes at the start of the lesson (where I am returning marked work) to read my comments thoroughly and then two minutes to answer on their Post-it note. This can be made into a 'think, pair, share' activity as appropriate. You may ask specific individuals to share their Post-it note with the class.

This is one of my most useful tools (particularly close to exams) as I can turn to any pupil's page and see immediately where their strengths and weaknesses are in specific topics. For example, consider the topic of fractions. A pupil could be excellent at the questions involving addition and subtraction of simple fractions but poor at converting top-heavy answers to mixed numbers. The Post-it note would indicate: 'strong on +/−' and I would pose a few questions converting top-heavy fractions to mixed numbers (this serves to remind me of their specific weakness). If I simply had a mark in my mark-book then all it would tell me is that they got, for example 10/15, and I would need to go back through their individual books to find the specific area of mathematics in the topic that causes concern. In using the Post-it note system I know immediately the weakness; in other words it is not generalised by RAG rating or a mark or grade.

Pupils also find looking at their own page useful. I can see the pupils who are always 'pink' and those who are nearly always 'yellow'; I can see those who have strength in algebra but are weak at data handling; and so on. This allows me to support differentiation for future topics (particularly where prior knowledge is needed) and to personalise their learning and revision plans as necessary. It also serves as an excellent tool when meeting with parents. It is simple and yet provides all of the information I need, much more than a mark-book as it actually shows pupils' work and questions/areas that they need to develop further.

Using this or a similar style ensures that work is not marked and then forgotten about. It is active marking. In other words, if pupils make errors they are actively encouraged to correct them and, moreover, to ensure they understand the topic. This prevents a piece of work being marked and then nothing ever really happening as a consequence of the marking; that is, work being marked and never looked at again, just becoming a mark in a mark-book.

The example in Figure 6.4 shows that pupil X demonstrated a very good understanding of recurring decimals and surds (indicated by T+). The questions extend their thinking further. The pink Post-it note relating to interior angles demonstrates that they completed the work on target and showed an understanding of finding, for example, missing angles solely with numbers, but need to further extend to problems that involve algebra and the question focuses on this. The yellow Post-it note shows a weakness in rearranging formulae (indicated by T–), with the concern being formulae involving 'squared terms'. The Post-it note gives an example and then asks pupil X to complete three simple problems. This will then be followed up to ensure that pupil X has a clear understanding of the process. When pupil X comes to prepare for an assessment then we need to ensure that they are confident at rearranging formulae; turning to their A4 page quickly shows the area of weakness, i.e. squared terms and fully completing the question (remembering to square root).

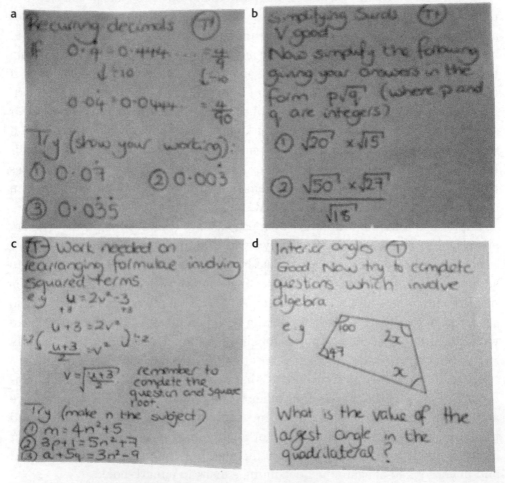

Figure 6.4 An example of active marking: an extract for pupil X. Post-it notes (a) and (b) are green, Post-it note (c) is yellow and Post-it note (d) is pink.

Do you correct every error?

There is no need to correct every error in full (always indicate whether a question is incorrect). Pick one or two questions and model the correct solution. If a pupil had got the majority of questions wrong you could otherwise be there forever. Ensure that as part of the commentary you set them a review task so that you can ensure they have read your corrections. It may be that they still cannot actually do the review task (despite your corrections) in which case they will need to arrange a time with you to discuss it so that you can support them further in this topic.

Do you correct spelling mistakes?

Highlighting spelling and grammatical errors is an important part of developing mathematical literacy. Ensure that you correct any errors and ask pupils to review these (otherwise you have corrected them and they take little notice which effectively has wasted your time!).

How often do you mark?

The frequency with which you mark or assess work is important. If you teach a full timetable during the week, then it is impossible to quality mark every piece of work done by a pupil in the way described above (unless you want to spend every evening and weekend marking!). So the trick is to carefully select the pieces of work that are going to provide you with enough information on the performance of pupils in particular topics. If for certain pupils you need to clarify understanding you may choose to review earlier work completed by that individual. Work should be regularly marked and, more importantly, marked close to the time of submission. For example, if you collect books in and mark work completed one month earlier the feedback loses its relevance and therefore its impact on learning.

Self-assessment and peer assessment

Both self-assessment and peer assessment are essential parts of the learning process. They are only effective if they are done well. Pupils need training in this process. For example, you cannot simply ask pupils to mark another pupil's work and then just call it peer assessment. Pupils need guidance and structure.

Self-assessment is where pupils assess their own learning. This would typically be against success criteria in achieving learning outcomes. Commonly pupils self-mark their work. This provides them with immediate quantitative feedback on their performance on a given topic. Pupils are sometimes then asked to traffic light this performance as red, amber or green. I ask this question: 'How do you know that just because they happen to get the correct numerical answer their method is correct?' For this reason, if you ask pupils to self-assess, ensure that you later review this for quality-control purposes. Alternatively, select a few key questions to review as a class, which pupils then self-assess focusing on key steps and processes. Ensure that pupils assess their own progress not only against the correct numerical answer but also against the correct mathematical procedure. This offers them more support and guidance in assessing their own work. If pupils have used the correct process for the few questions you collectively review, then they have most likely used this process for the remainder (therefore marking by response alone for the other questions is fine).

In self-assessing (as with peer assessment) the purpose needs to be clear. It is not about simply getting 'x out of 10' but about thinking about the learning process and encouraging pupils to take responsibility for their own learning. Have they met the success criteria? How do they know? Have they made errors? Can they identify what these are? What do they need to do to take their learning to the next step? Pupils should be able to answer all of these questions when they self-assess, otherwise it simply becomes an exercise in marking and the value on learning is lost.

Peer assessment needs to be conducted carefully. For a start, some pupils don't like others writing in their books; be considerate here. Ensure that pupils know the boundaries of what they write. It may be that for peer assessment you produce a little tick sheet of the success criteria linked to a given activity and you ask the peer assessor to write their name on and then to tick off whether they think each success criteria has been met; this can be glued into the pupils book.

For example, in plotting straight-line graphs the success criteria for peer marking may be:

- pencil has been used
- axes have been drawn and are correctly labelled (e.g. x and y)
- the correct scale has been used on the axes
- the table of values (x,y) has been included and the values are correct
- points are plotted in pencil accurately and then joined with a straight line that extends beyond the points
- each line is labelled with the correct equation.

As pupils peer mark a question you would ensure that you circulate and glance quickly at the work. As with self-assessment, peer marking needs quality control and so you need to take books in and ensure that the marking is correct. On the sheet you issue you can add a section for learning comments. These need to be developed over time, but will link to the success criteria.

Two stars and a wish is a commonly used peer assessment technique for this purpose. Pupils are asked to highlight two positives about the work and then to identify one area for improvement. Again, key to this activity is the reference to success criteria. In completing a peer assessment activity both the assessor and the assessed should gain from the process. In addition to writing down their thoughts on another pupil's work, I always ask pupils to note in their own book (or wherever you choose) whose work they have peer assessed and what they learnt from the activity. For example, did they assess a pupil's work in which more steps in working had been shown? Did they really understand the importance of working when they reviewed work with none? Did they learn the value of diagrammatical representation? Did they gain from the experience something that they had not done in their own work? Once pupils have assessed a partner's work it is important to allow a short time for discussion among the peers and then to invite pairs to share anything that they gained from the experience. Adding learning value to the activity is important to its success.

If you are new to peer assessment and you want to develop pupils skills in assessing their own or others' learning then pre-prepare a sample of work with a range of questions on it. Ask pupils individually to assess the work, ask them to share their thoughts with a peer and then ask them to form small groups and discuss their thoughts on the work and areas for improvement. These tasks serve two purposes. First, they encourage pupils to look at work, spot misconceptions or focus on whether mathematical processes have been correctly applied, and the second is that they develop their explicit assessment skills, that is, where they focus on setting targets for improvement. As you regroup as a class you can ask key questions to develop assessment skills.

Reflection

Reflection is part of self-assessment; it is a metacognitive phase in learning. Part of this thinking process is to think about what they have learnt and, of course, any mistakes or misconceptions. We are all familiar with the phrase 'we learn from our mistakes'. Well, we do. If pupils make mistakes in their learning then they learn most from unpicking them and understanding where they went wrong. Create an environment where it is safe to make a mistake.

Making mistakes simply means you are learning faster.

(Weston H. Agor)

The important part of the reflection process is that if pupils have made an error then they highlight it and identify how they can correct it, noting their thought process. This gives you an insight into their understanding.

The next stage in the reflection process is setting targets and identifying 'next steps' in learning. Encouraging metacognition is an essential part of the learning process. Reflection is discussed in more detail in Chapter 4.

Mini-assessment points

Mini-assessment points are probably most commonly referred to as progress checks. Outstanding teachers constantly and regularly (whether explicitly or not) check the progress pupils are making towards learning outcomes at key points in the learning process. They then adapt their teaching as necessary. In an outstanding lesson all pupils make progress.

Mini-assessment activities are short. They allow a teacher to assess the class as a whole and mini-whiteboards are an excellent tool for whole-class assessment. Types of mini-assessment activities are discussed in Chapters 2–4.

Use the mini-assessments to ensure that success criteria are being met. Ask the pupils what the success criteria were for the activity and ask them how this has allowed them to work towards the learning outcomes. Encouraging pupils to think in this way rather than being told the success criteria for an activity keeps their minds focused on the underlying mathematical concepts.

Mini-assessments do not have to be reviews of each activity, where you read out answers and pupils mark them. This becomes tedious. They can be two simple questions that allow you to assess progress. They also don't have to be done at the end of an activity. You may get a feeling that pupils are not going along the right path and so you stop the activity and add a progress check. You can then redirect your teaching or intervene as appropriate. This may be where you differentiate and have some pupils working with you on one table and others working independently according to the result of the progress check (this will be further discussed in Chapter 7).

Mini-assessments can be referenced to grades, but be careful on your grade criteria, as discussed earlier in this chapter. Is there real benefit at this stage in asking pupils to grade themselves? What purpose will it serve?

The final assessment activity

The final assessment activity or progress check is the plenary. This is discussed in full in Chapter 4. The main point to make here is that you should always include a final assessment opportunity or closing activity. This should be where pupils can demonstrate the skills they have acquired during the lesson and assess whether they have met the learning outcomes.

Summary

Assessment is a key feature of an outstanding lesson and a powerful tool to drive learning. It helps learners to know how to improve and promotes an understanding of measurable success criteria and learning outcomes. Embedding assessment for learning into your lessons, involving pupils and encouraging them to take responsibility for their learning and reflect on the 'next steps' are central to an outstanding lesson.
Assessment can take many forms and it is important to:

- know whether the assessment you are doing is *as*, *of* or *for* learning
- ensure that each activity you do builds in a mini-assessment opportunity
- use self-assessment and peer assessment in a guided way to support learning
- adapt your teaching as a result of the assessment points
- monitor and track pupil progress on a regular basis and use this to provide informative data that support learning and teaching.

CHAPTER 7

Thirty different minds?

Personalising learning is important. In any class (even those that are set) there will be a range of abilities and a range of learning preferences. It is important that we as educators are aware of these when setting learning activities. After all, remember that in front of you are thirty (approximately) individuals: individuals who like different things, individuals who have different life experiences, individuals with different levels of confidence and individuals who think differently. Through differentiation we can personalise the learning experience using different strategies and take some strides to making the learning of mathematics accessible for all. It is the strategies we use that define differentiation.

Why is the lack of differentiation often highlighted in lesson observation feedback? Let's be honest – what we really are asking is why teachers don't always differentiate. There can be many different reasons for this, including:

- sticking rigidly to schemes of work or curriculum maps in order to ensure that content is delivered for examinations
- the perceived workload that is equated to the word differentiation
- concern about losing control when several different activities are happening at the same time
- that mathematics groups/classes are commonly set by ability and therefore all pupils are similar, which means that there is no need to differentiate
- lack of training in effective differentiation strategies.

Yet the benefits of differentiating bring an enhanced learning environment where pupils experience quality learning, resulting in increased levels of motivation, behaviour and progress. At the same time, as teachers we have to recognise that while too little or no differentiation can lead to all pupils receiving the same mathematical diet (whole-class teaching) the converse of too much differentiation can lead to a frenzied environment which can appear quite chaotic. Therefore it is important to achieve a healthy balance on the differentiation continuum. Outstanding teachers plan for differentiation and don't create excessive amounts of work for themselves, but use simple techniques and strategies to ensure that they differentiate resources or that they differentiate their approach. As with any form of teaching, taking a varied approach is important in securing levels of interest and engagement from pupils.

Imagine you are asked to teach addition to a 5-year-old and a 12-year-old. This is all the information you are given. I have no doubt you would immediately assess each individual and make assumptions. Most likely for the 5-year-old you would think of using props such as counting blocks and plan for addition of single-digit number, and for the 12-year-old a more complex sum using pen and paper, 2561 − 239 for example. In its most simplistic form this is differentiation. You are assessing the pupils and then ensuring that the task is matched to the needs and ability of the learner.

There are different types of differentiation, and in this chapter we look at different strategies that can be used to differentiate the learning experience in our classrooms. The very best teachers implicitly combine the differentiation techniques rather than using one form explicitly.

Differentiation by ability

This is perhaps the most common form of differentiation. How you differentiate by ability is extremely important. Pre-assigning pupils to different ability categories based on prior assessment (perhaps assessments that were used to set the class) for differentiation purposes can be misleading. For example, a pupil may have performed poorly in the previous year's end of term examination, but they could have excelled on the algebra questions and done poorly on geometry, data handling and the application of number, leading to an overall score of below average. If you were completing a unit on algebra and pre-assigned this pupil to the lower ability cohort then the pupil could easily become demotivated and disengage with the learning as this is an area in which they are competent.

The same caution should be applied when using target grades to assign pupils to differentiated materials. This can have a ceiling effect on pupil's performance.

If you use this type of differentiation technique then use mini-assessments at key points during the lesson to allow differentiation by ability. If a pupil has done well in a particular mini-assessment (remember, these need only be two or three different styles of question), then they will be assigned a more challenging activity. This makes differentiation by ability more dynamic and has much more power over pre-assigned performance.

Examples of worksheets where differentiation by ability is used are shown in Figures 7.1, 7.2 and 7.3.

Label the sides (in relation to angles *a*, *b* and *c* in each diagram) opposite, adjacent and hypotenuse

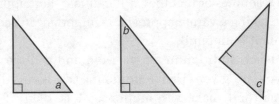

For each of the following find the length of the side labelled with a letter:

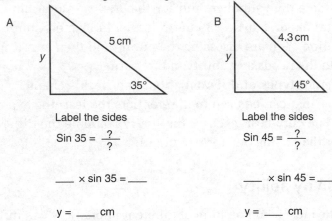

A
5 cm
y
35°

Label the sides

Sin 35 = $\dfrac{?}{?}$

____ × sin 35 = ____

y = ____ cm

B
4.3 cm
y
45°

Label the sides

Sin 45 = $\dfrac{?}{?}$

____ × sin 45 = ____

y = ____ cm

C
12 cm
x
30°

D
p
7 cm
50°

Find the height of the ramp *h*:

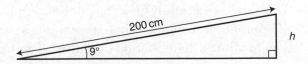

200 cm
h
9°

Figure 7.1 Trigonometry worksheet X.

For each of the following find the length of the side labelled with a letter:

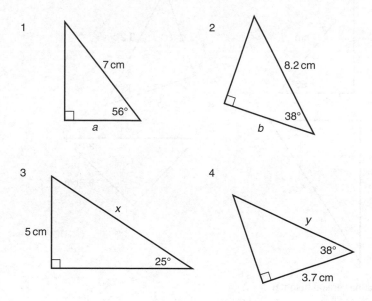

5   A ramp with triangular cross-section makes an angle of 9° to the horizontal.
    The ramp is 200 cm long. Draw a diagram and calculate the height of the ramp.

6   Calculate the vertical height *h* of the length of the triangle. Explain your answer.

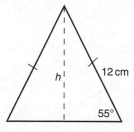

Figure 7.2 Trigonometry worksheet Y.

103

For each of the following find the length of the side labelled with a letter:

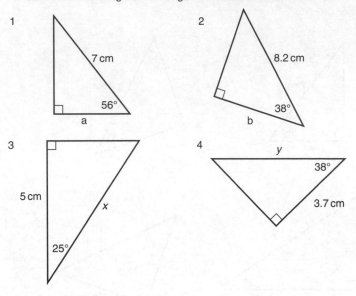

1   7 cm   56°   a

2   8.2 cm   38°   b

3   5 cm   x   25°

4   y   38°   3.7 cm

5   Find the vertical height h:

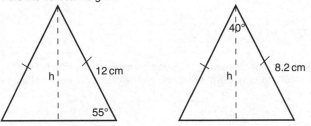

12 cm   h   55°

40°   h   8.2 cm

6   A footpath is 230 m long.
It goes straight uphill at an angle of 25° to the horizontal.
The lower end of the footpath is 87 metres above sea level.

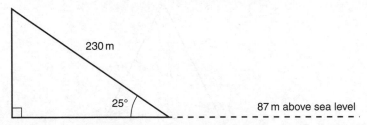

230 m   25°   87 m above sea level

Calculate the height above sea level of the upper end of the footpath.

Figure 7.3 Trigonometry worksheet Z.

104

The worksheets progress in level from X to Z. The questions for the more able pupils offer increasing levels of challenge and the questions for the less able offer more practice at questions that ensure they embed the method. All worksheets have questions that involve application of the concept, but again the level of support and the complexity of the questions vary depending upon the level of challenge offered.

Differentiation by gender

Much research indicates different learning patterns and behaviours between girls and boys. Girls apparently tend to be more empathetic, neat and sharing and boys tend to be more active and competitive and want quick solutions. This is probably something that we can relate to. Remember, though, that this is only a generalisation, but it should be something that you are aware of when designing learning opportunities. For example, you may create a competitive environment for boys where they compete against each other and the clock to find a solution to a problem. My personal opinion is that you differentiate to the individual and individuals through knowing your learners rather than by classification. I know, for instance, many girls who are competitive and have the traits associated to the male learner.

Differentiation by resource

Differentiating a resource can be done in several different ways. This is generally where pupils have similar resources. For example, in a lesson on data analysis you may have several different data sets (some easier to handle than others) which offer different levels of challenge but which have the same learning outcome, such as finding the mean, median and mode.

Example 7.1

- Find the mean, median and mode for the following: 2, 5, 2, 8, 6, 20, 3, 8, 8
- Find the mean, median and mode for the following: 12.2, 14.7, 5.1, 6.3, 5.1, 18.7, 12.9, 18.7.

In the two examples pupils are asked to use the same mathematical processes but the numbers they are using are different and it is clear that the second example offers more challenge (particularly in finding the median as it will lie between two values).

Other simple examples to illustrate this concept are given in Examples 7.2 and 7.3.

Example 7.2
Expand the following expressions:

- $3(2a + 4)$
- $-4(9 - 3a)$

The second example provides a greater challenge as it includes the multiplication of negative numbers and has the algebraic term placed second inside the bracket; however, both questions utilise the same underlying mathematical concept and involve multiplying a single term over a bracket.

Example 7.3
- Divide 225 by 15
- A sweet shop owner has to place 225 sweets equally into 15 bags. How many sweets are in each bag?

In the first problem we are telling the pupil the operation to use, i.e. division and in the second we are expecting the pupil to determine that the correct operation is division before they tackle the calculation. The sum is obviously the same in each and therefore the mathematical calculation is identical, but in the second question pupils are expected to apply their knowledge.

Questions can also be differentiated by the level of support a pupil is given. For example, consider Example 7.4, where the first question offers a greater level of challenge and the second more support through scaffolding. In both cases pupils achieve the same outcomes but the level of support offers the differentiation. Examples are shown in Figures 7.4 and 7.5.

Example 7.4

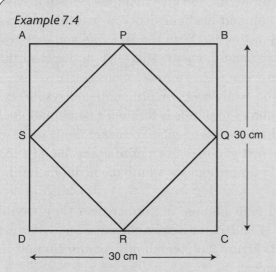

Figure 7.4 Application of Pythagoras.

In the application of Pythagoras for more able pupils we would pose the question direct:

> In Figure 7.4 the square PQRS is made by joining the midpoints of the square ABCD. The square ABCD has sides of length 30 cm. Calculate the length of one side of the square PQRS.

Where pupils require further support scaffolding may be needed. In this case we may break the question down, encouraging pupils to develop their reasoning and reduce the question to a simple one involving Pythagoras, as shown in Figure 7.5.

- What is the midpoint of a line?
- What is the length of CQ and QB? Explain your answer.
- Sketch the triangle RCQ and label the length of the sides that you know.
- Calculate the length of RQ.

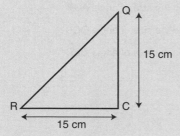

Figure 7.5 Reducing the question to a simple question involving Pythagoras.

Thirty different minds?

Support can also mean the level of input that you give to pupils. You may have those who need additional extension and challenge so you may plant ideas with them first through effective questioning. With the less able you may use questioning to develop their learning and to ensure that they understand the underlying mathematical concept.

How do you assign pupils to the worksheets or differentiated resources? The very best way of assigning resources to pupils is through a combination of pupil choice, your judgement and mini-assessments. For example, if we take the worksheets on circle theorems, first you may use a mini-assessment (using whiteboards to allow you to see all pupil responses simultaneously) including the questions shown in Figure 7.6.

If a pupil gets questions 1 and 2 in Figure 7.6 correct then they would complete worksheet A (Figure 7.7) and if they only got question 1 correct they would complete worksheet B (Figure 7.8), which offers more support in developing and using the basic concept.

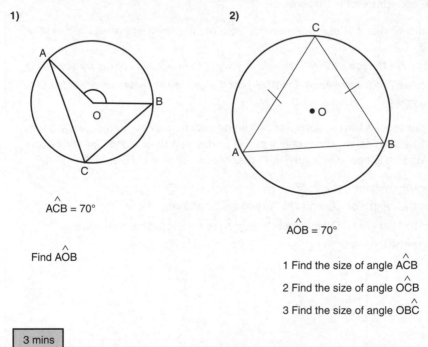

1)

$\hat{ACB} = 70°$

Find $\hat{AOB}$

2)

$\hat{AOB} = 70°$

1 Find the size of angle $\hat{ACB}$

2 Find the size of angle $\hat{OCB}$

3 Find the size of angle $\hat{OBC}$

3 mins

Figure 7.6 A simple mini-assessment.

1 Angle $A\hat{O}B = 56°$

   Find angle $A\hat{C}B$

2 Angle $A\hat{C}B = 31.5°$

   Find angle $A\hat{O}B$

3 Angle $A\hat{C}B = 21°$

   Find the REFLEX angle $A\hat{O}B$

4 Angle $A\hat{C}B = 48°$

   Find angle $A\hat{O}B$

5 Angle $A\hat{C}B = 56°$

   Find angle $A\hat{O}B$

6 Angle $A\hat{O}B = 97°$

   Find angle $A\hat{C}B$

7 Angle $A\hat{O}B = 70°$

   Find angle $A\hat{C}B$

8a What type of triangle is triangle AOC?

8b Triangle AOC and BOC are said to be _____

8c Angle $A\hat{O}B = 102°$. Find the size of angle $A\hat{C}B$.

8d What is the size of angle $O\hat{C}B$?

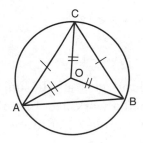

Figure 7.7 Worksheet A: the angle subtended at the centre of a circle is twice the angle subtended at the circumference.

1 Angle $A\hat{C}B = 48°$

Find angles $A\hat{O}B$ and $O\hat{C}B$

2 Angle $A\hat{C}B = 60°$

Find angles $A\hat{O}B$ and $O\hat{B}C$

3 Angle $A\hat{O}B = 74°$

Find angles $A\hat{C}B$ and $A\hat{D}B$

4 ABC is an isosceles triangle, $A\hat{O}B = 102°$

Find size of angle $O\hat{B}C$

5 Angle $A\hat{O}B = 126°$. Angle $O\hat{A}C = 51°$

Find angles $A\hat{C}B$ and $O\hat{B}C$

6 Calculate the sizes of angles $A\hat{B}C$ and $A\hat{D}C$

Figure 7.8 Worksheet B: the angle subtended at the centre of a circle is twice the angle subtended at the circumference.

A further example using inequalities is a mini-assessment that includes questions such as:

1) $3a - 7 > 2$
2) $4m + 3 < 12$
3) $7 + 2c > -15$
4) $5 - 3p < -4$

If a pupil gets all the questions and method correct then they would be assigned a worksheet that offers more challenge and develops questions such as in Example 7.3 or further to those such as in Example 7.6.

Example 7.5
1) $3(b-1) + 4(b+2) < 40$
2) $5(n+3) - 3(n+3) > 26$
3) $4(m+5) + 2(3m-5) > 50$
4) $3(2b+1) - 4(b+3) > 9$
5) $10(4b-3) - 5(2b-20) < 250$

Example 7.6
1) $4(a-2) > 2(a+2)$
2) $3(x+2) > 2(x-1)$
3) $3(y-1) + 7 > 2(y+1)$

More able pupils can be extended to representing inequalities and solutions on a graph or to questions that apply the skills, such as:

> *A rectangle has a length of (2a + 4) cm and a width of 10 cm. The area is greater than 300 cm². What is the minimum length of the rectangle (to the nearest cm)?*

If a pupil struggled and answered only question one of the mini-assessment correctly or showed little comprehension of the concept, then you would assign them worksheets that allow pupils to practise developing the basic concepts and ensure that you target your support to this individual. If the outcome of the mini-assessment reveals that several pupils struggled and others completed the questions, then group them together according to ability. This way you can target your support in a more effective way and have greater impact on developing the learning in your classroom. If you don't want to produce three or more separate worksheets then differentiate through the question pathway that pupils take, but ensure that all pupils experience a variety of questions. For example, don't leave your lower-ability students always doing the first few questions and never experiencing the using and applying questions, which develop their mathematical thinking. Always have high expectations and never aim too low for pupils. As self-selection is an important part of the learning process allow pupils to make their own choice but guide them where necessary.

Differentiation by activity or task

This is different from differentiating a resource. In differentiating an activity or a task we have separate and distinct activities or work stations. The important feature when differentiating by task is that all of the tasks link together, sequence the learning and work towards the learning outcomes. One group of pupils may be asked to make a podcast or another may be asked to write a Twitter feed or others to produce a newspaper article or watch a video clip and comment. The key concept is challenge and choice.

An alternative take on differentiation by task is where pupils are asked in groups to investigate different areas of mathematics in different ways, which are then brought together to complete the picture. This has been discussed in the jigsaw activity in Chapter 3.

However you choose to differentiate by task, maximise learning potential by carefully matching the activities to the learning preference of the individual and to the activity you feel they will most benefit from.

Differentiation by learning preference

Learning styles have been discussed in Chapter 3. The main point to address here is that it is important to ensure that your lesson or series of lessons draw from a variety of activities that require application of the different learning styles, visual, auditory or kinaesthetic or a combination of these. In Chapter 3 we discussed different learning styles and activities suited to each learning preference. Be conscious that all pupils should experience different types of learning (otherwise we reinforce one particular learning style and they find it more difficult to access other styles). This can be combined with differentiation by task by having different activities or work stations that suit the different learning styles or combinations of learning preferences.

Differentiation by outcome

Differentiation by outcome is where all pupils complete the same task and the various pupil outcomes provide the differentiation. In other words, pupils' responses at different levels determine the differentiation. While differentiation by outcome does allow direct comparison of learners, it is not considered best practice when it comes to differentiation, but is referred to here in order for the distinction between different types of differentiation to be made. Simply using a worksheet or textbook is not a good example of differentiation by outcome as this doesn't personalise the learning and is really what teachers who don't differentiate do. To ensure that differentiation by outcome is successful and used to best effect, then the activity needs to be open ended, such as an investigation.

In differentiating by outcome you may have different graded outcomes against which pupils can assess their progress. For example, in expanding two brackets to produce a quadratic expression the learning outcomes might be:

- I can expand and simplify the product of two simple linear expressions such as $(a + 2)(a + 3)$.
- I can expand and simplify the product of any two simple linear expressions where the coefficients are greater than one such as $(2a - 7)(3a - 4)$.
- I can expand and simplify any linear expressions such as $(2q - p)(3p - 2q)$.
- I can apply to word problems and select the appropriate method.

The outcome determines the level at which pupils are working and we can see natural progression from one success criteria to the next.

Differentiation by interest

This is something that outstanding teachers do naturally and really is common sense. If you are to engage a young mind then the very best way is to bring the mathematics alive with something they are interested in. Consider a class of boys; it would be unlikely that they would be interested in designing a statistical survey to find out about the most popular clothes designer, but bring statistics alive with football and suddenly their interest is awakened. Matching resources to pupil's interests or engaging students with interesting real-life examples is an excellent tool for motivating learners and contextualising the learning.

Differentiation by grouping

Differentiation by grouping really allows for you to ensure that pupils of a similar ability offer each other support and that you are able to target your support to particular groups. You may set a challenging task to one group and then set a similar task, but with a more structured approach or greater degree of scaffolding, to pupils who are of a lower ability. Grouping should be dynamic and, again, not preformed but formed on the outcomes of mini-assessments completed during the lesson. This ensures that pupils are supported by their peers in ability groupings according to the task.

Within a group there are different roles, including, for example, scribe, researcher, leader, time keeper and spokesperson. Differentiation by role means assigning different individuals to different roles to either develop their strength in a particular role or encourage their confidence in another role.

Differentiation through questioning

Questioning is discussed in detail in Chapter 5. Questioning is perhaps the most powerful tool in differentiation in a classroom. Using Bloom's taxonomy to ensure challenging and effective questioning is a critical component in the learning process.

Home learning

You have completed a lesson. You know that not all pupils achieved the same learning outcome. Some may have struggled more than others. Why, therefore, would you set them all the same work to complete at home? If you did, the same learners who struggled in the lesson would struggle with the home learning and the pupils who excelled would no doubt complete the work very quickly. If you therefore set the same task to all pupils then it becomes unfair and can demotivate.

The same principles applied during the lesson to differentiate the learning experience and ensure it is accessible to all need to be applied to the home learning. This is why many schools opt for a more open task or project that uses the mathematical skills developed over a series of lessons and that can be developed according to the depth of mathematical ability of the pupil.

If you do set task-based home learning then ensure that the resource is either at different levels or has different pathways to support different learners. This then allows for all pupils to become accustomed to completing studies at home and ensures they achieve success. Mismatching the home learning to the pupil's ability can lead to frustration and home learning not being accessible.

Before you set home learning ensure that you are clear on its purpose. Is it to reinforce concepts developed during the lesson and therefore further practice (or more of the same)? Is it a single question that requires pupils to apply the concepts learned during the lesson? Is it a mini-investigation? Does it require independent research? All of these are simple to differentiate using the techniques described above. For example, consider home learning that required the application of knowledge following a lesson on Pythagoras.

Question A

A 12 foot ladder is placed against the wall of a house as shown in Figure 7.9. The ladder reaches 9.5 feet up the wall. How far is the foot of the ladder from the base of the wall?

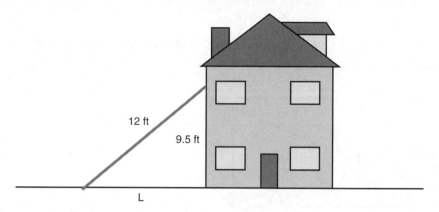

Figure 7.9 Ladder against a wall problem.

Question B

Find the shortest distance between two points a and b with coordinates (3,4) and (−4,1) respectively, as shown in Figure 7.10.

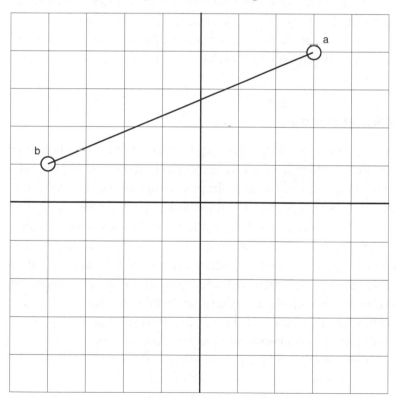

Figure 7.10 Find the shortest distance between the coordinates.

Question C

A cuboid is 3 metres by 5 metres by 15 metres, as shown in Figure 7.11. Find the length of the diagonal across the cuboid.

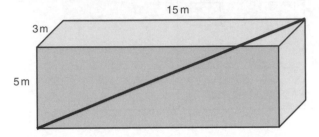

Figure 7.11 Find the length of the diagonal across the cuboid.

I have used only a single question to demonstrate questions that progress in the level of challenge and application (and, of course, you will most likely set more). In its simplest form this ensures differentiation by ability and allows you to assign pupils to a given challenge for their home learning that they can access. Promoting success is important. If you do want all pupils to complete the same activity then I advocate the use of more open-ended or investigative-style questions, which pupils can then develop to the best of their own personal ability.

Special educational needs

It is not my intention to delve into the very expert field of special educational needs (SEN). There are a multitude of texts and research dedicated to particular educational needs and indeed most schools have a dedicated SEN coordinator, or SENCO, who specialises in this area. They are best placed to offer you expert advice and helpful hints for ensuring that pupils with SEN are able to access learning. Indeed, just because a pupil has a specific SEN does not mean they will require the same support as an individual with the same SEN and the differences within an SEN category are often wide. As with all pupils, it is important to personalise learning to the individual rather than to label them with SEN and a textbook approach. Find what works best and use it to scaffold the learning. Communication with parents also helps. Parents can support their child's learning in their home environment and also provide you with excellent knowledge and provide a different perspective on their child's needs.

The types of SEN that we most commonly come across in schools are attention deficit hyperactivity disorder (ADHD), autistic spectrum disorder (ASD) and Asperger's syndrome (a form of autism), physical impairments and speech and language disorders. In addition are specific learning difficulties including dyslexia, dyspraxia and dyscalculia. Pupils may, of course, have a combination of SEN and /or specific learning difficulties, which is why personalisation is so important to ensure that they can fully access the learning and reach their full potential in mathematics.

Pupils with dyslexia generally struggle with decoding and comprehension, which means it can be difficult for them to understand word problems in mathematics. In addition, they may reverse symbols such as < and >. The technical language can also be difficult for them to master. However, pupils with dyslexia typically recognise patterns and using this to support learning can help them access mathematics. Help pupils to see the bigger picture and try to use real-life scenarios or comparisons where possible. When starting problems always ensure that pupils with dyslexia are fully aware of what the task is asking of them.

Dyscalculia is a learning difficulty specific to learning mathematics and in particular number. Try to make learning fun and accessible. Work with the pupil and their teaching assistant (if one is allocated). Help pupils to over-learn the basics and try, where possible, to use concrete objects and flow diagrams, limiting lengthy methods copied from a board. Link learning to real-life situations and try, where possible, to create a multisensory environment. For pupils with dyscalculia making connections between mathematical concepts and processes can help to support their learning.

Whatever the specific learning need or difficulty, remember that all pupils are individuals and information is power. So arm yourself with as much information as you can from all the different sources around you: teaching colleagues, your past experience, the school SENCO, the teaching assistant and the pupil's parents. Perhaps the most important thing that you need to do is work with the pupil to find what works best for them.

Gifted and talented learners

Schools often label pupils as gifted or talented in a particular area or subject. How they arise at these labels is sometimes dubious and how often do they review pupils on the 'list'? What are the criteria and who decides? Would a pupil labelled as gifted in one school be labelled as gifted in another? I am not sure I agree particularly with labelling a child as gifted in mathematics because children will often exhibit 'giftedness' in different areas within the subject.

However, that is only my opinion, so let us continue with how we cater for the gifted learner in mathematics. Often people say we should enhance the learning of gifted mathematicians through enrichment, but shouldn't the mathematics of all pupils be enhanced through enrichment? Shouldn't we offer all pupils who show a genuine interest the opportunity to experience the wonders of mathematics through a rich and challenging curriculum?

Rich tasks are probably one of the best ways to allow all learners, including those who are described as gifted in mathematics, to shine to their full potential. NRICH coins this nicely through 'low threshold, high ceiling (LTHC)' tasks.

> *A LTHC mathematical activity is one which pretty well everyone in the group can begin, and then work on at their own level of engagement, but which has lots of possibilities for the participants to do much more challenging mathematics.*

(http://nrich.maths.org/7701)

As discussed in the referenced article, these types of activities (as with all rich tasks) mean that all pupils are working on the same problem but differentiation is through their outcome. They can develop the task according to their given level of mathematical ability. It is not necessarily offering different levels of content but developing the depth of thinking skills. This gives more able mathematicians the opportunity to shine (http://nrich.maths.org/7701 has ideas for LTHC tasks from the primary phase through to sixth form).

If you choose to set the same worksheet or a task that is closed to all pupils then gifted or more able pupils will be most likely to finish quickly, so always have prepared an extension activity that challenges and develops their thinking, allowing them to gain experience of the topic in greater depth (not just more of the same). I think challenging more able pupils with greater depth is the best way forward. Often schools accelerate the curriculum and cover topics more quickly with more able pupils (as commonly schools set pupils into groups by mathematics ability with the more able in the top set). However, if we are to create mathematicians of the future, better is to take the time and opportunity to study topics in greater depth and to really deepen understanding and challenge thinking.

Summary

Differentiation is an essential feature of an outstanding lesson. After all, if you don't differentiate then you are assuming that all learners are the same, which we know is certainly not the case, even in similar-ability grouping. Through differentiation we teach a concept and ensure that we meet the different learning needs of all pupils in the class. It does not mean that you have to spend hour upon hour creating multiple resources, but simply that you think about the learners in your classroom and that you adapt resources or activities to ensure that they can all access the learning.

While we have discussed the common types of differentiation as separate entities, the very best teachers naturally combine different styles to ensure they meet the needs of the learners. To facilitate learning effectively you need to think about which type or combination of differentiation strategies is going to be most suited to the lesson you develop. Summarised below are the main types of differentiation discussed in this chapter:

- Differentiation by task or activity: pupils have separate and distinct activities that all work towards achieving the learning outcomes.
- Differentiation by resource: pupils are all using the same concept to answer the same basic question (for example, 'find the mean'), but at different levels of challenge through, for example, the numbers or wording used.
- Differentiation by ability: pupils are assigned different levels of work or worksheets (based on the outcomes of mini-assessments) in which questions are different.
- Differentiation by outcome: all pupils complete the same open-ended task, but the different pupil outcomes determine the level of differentiation.
- Differentiation by grouping: use peer-ability groupings and further differentiate through role and support.
- Differentiation by learning preference: differentiate activities or resources to accommodate the different learning styles (visual, auditory, kinaesthetic).
- Differentiation by interest: adapt questions or resources to ensure that they appeal to the interests of different learners.
- Differentiation through questioning: use different styles and levels of questioning to challenge pupils effectively.

CHAPTER 8

The classroom environment

Classroom displays

The classroom should be a multisensory environment and an environment that supports learning. Look around your classroom. What do you see? Sit in one of the chairs at the back of your classroom. Now what do you see? When was the last time you changed your displays? If they are tired or if they have been up for some time, then they probably have little or no impact on the pupils in your classroom. They probably look past them and you probably do too. Displays are a powerful and yet often underused tool in education and can take many forms. In this section we will look at some different styles of display.

Displaying pupils' work

Pupils love to see their work displayed. One of the displays in your classroom should be dedicated to pupils' work. This doesn't always have to be completed work that is specifically for display purposes; it can be work in progress, photocopies of material or photographs of work or projects as they develop (a start-to-finish concept). Photographs of pupils working on different activities, or screenshots of videos that they produce, add a different dimension to displays and they are easy to do (taken as part of one of your normal lessons). The important thing is to ensure that the work is regularly rotated, updated and kept fresh. Having the same work displayed in July that was completed in October is not a good use of display. Regularly changing the displays means that pupils will look at them and if the displays are not of specific display work then this is easy to do as part of your day-to-day teaching – just have a camera or iPad on hand to photograph pupils' work in progress or pupils working together as a team.

Posters

Pre-prepared posters are often used in classrooms and, most likely, if you look around your own or a colleague's classroom they are the same posters as they were last year. Chances are that they look a little tired. This is when displays become pointless. You may as well use wallpaper. So, if you must use posters then make them work for you. Add mathematical purpose. This may be something as simple as placing different mathematical challenges around the poster (simple A4 pieces of paper work well). The posters can be used as part of one of your lessons with pupils using the information in them as part of their learning process. Alternatively, a nice activity is to place Post-it notes (named for each pupil) around the poster and then during the lesson pupils are asked to go and get their specific challenge, place their answer on the back of their Post-it note and put it back. You can then select as part of the plenary or assessment opportunity some of the Post-it notes to review. You can mark these Post-it notes and return to pupils for their books or for your review folder (as discussed in Chapter 6). For example, for a poster on the laws of indices you may have Post-it notes around it with simple questions such as $a^3 \times a^7$ for some pupils and more challenging questions for others, such as $8a^{-5} \times - 7a^{-9}$. This allows for differentiation and the display has become an active part of the lesson. Rotate posters as a department. Laminate them if possible so that they stay in good condition and then swap them among team members when you refresh your display or need to use the poster as part of a lesson.

An alternative is to enlarge A3 questions and display them around the room on different coloured paper. Pupils can be assigned to these individually (with more than one pupil going to the same poster), in pairs or in groups and work on different problems highlighted as areas for improvement at the assessment points. Pupils can then discuss their findings in groups and attempt to work towards a solution. This type of activity further allows for differentiation.

Word walls

Word walls are common displays in mathematics classrooms, on which mathematical words are shown. But what's the point? What do pupils gain simply from seeing a word on a wall? Word or vocabulary awareness is one reason and so is ensuring that you support the school literacy policy, but do pupils really look at them and do you ever use them? Better is to make the word walls interactive. So add a definition. Place the word in large lettering with the definition and a question underneath. Use these in your lesson. Add a piece of laminated coloured paper over the definition and then stick it (Velcro tabs are very good for this) over the definition. As part of a lesson you can ask pupils for the definition and then remove the coloured piece and see if they were correct. They can then complete the question. This makes the display interactive and part of the learning process. This can be a nice activity at the end of a lesson. It may be that certain pupils (based on the assessment evidence) need to work further on specific topics. In this way you may allocate five minutes at the start of the next lesson and ask pupils to go to specific words and complete the problems. Examples are shown in Figures 8.1 and 8.2.

MEDIAN

The median is the middle number when items are arranged in order of size

1) Find the median: 2, 7, 5, 4, 4, 1, 9

2) Find the median: 18, 31, 22, 25, 7, 14

Figure 8.1 An example of a card defining the *median value* for a word wall.

RECIPROCAL

The reciprocal of a is 1/a

Find the reciprocal of:

1) 2
2) 5
3) $\frac{2}{3}$
4) *b/a*

Figure 8.2 An example of a card defining *reciprocal* for a word wall.

The challenge board

This is an opportunity for you to set a mathematical problem that pupils can then post their answers to. The best solution can be placed in a prize draw or get house points if you operate a rewards system within the school. This doesn't have to be a learning activity within the lesson. It can be an activity that pupils take part in if they wish to.

Examples of problems include:

> *When I went to the supermarket I purchased four items. Three items were priced at £1.50, £3 and £4. The prices of the four items added together give the same number as when I multiplied all four prices together. What was the price of the fourth item?*

Alternatively, this board can be used to post interesting mathematical articles or interesting mathematical careers information or pupils can submit articles or mathematical challenges or interesting pieces for you to review and place on the board. Pupil involvement on this level is wonderful and it works. As this develops pupils can take responsibility for the board, but for it to work well it must be refreshed on a regular basis. I suggest weekly, or once every two weeks.

The question board

Keep a board clear and head it with a question mark. This can be where learners post information, things they have learnt or misconceptions they have overcome, or general questions that have arisen during the lesson and can be referred to at the mini-plenary or during the main plenary. A small whiteboard that you can wipe clean is a good resource.

The key is to make displays work and to ensure that they are not just a substitute for wallpaper. The very best displays are interactive and form part of the learning process. They provide interesting discussion points for pupils and they are used or referred to in the lesson. They don't have to be the perfectly coloured-in pieces of work in the very best handwriting (traditional display work) that nobody ever really looks at, or shiny new posters which look nice but are really only there to brighten the classroom wall. Pupils should come into your room and look at the displays for something new because they know (and, more importantly, come to expect) that you will change them regularly. That is, after all, their purpose, to be part of the learning culture and to promote independence and metacognition. If you don't have your own classroom, then try to take ownership of one of the displays in the classroom that you share or in the corridor. Once you make your displays more interactive you will inspire others to do the same and, most importantly, promote interest among pupils.

The classroom climate

Does your classroom promote a climate for learning? Whose voice is heard most often? If your face froze in its most common expression, what would it be? What is the most common phrase you use (and do you realise!)? Where do you commonly position yourself in the classroom?

The purpose of your classroom is to engage pupils with mathematics and creating a warm and positive learning environment can help to motivate pupils. Starting from the moment pupils walk through the door, smile and greet them by name. This is basic psychology. If we are smiled at then we tend to smile back and if we are referred to by name we tend to feel more valued. Occupy pupils who have arrived with bell work, as discussed in Chapter 2. This sets the tone.

It is harder to try to re-establish a routine or expectations part of the way through the year, so start from the very first day and if they don't come easy make sure you persevere. Relationships between the teacher and learner are important, but are also fragile. Be firm but fair. Respect is a two-way process. Make your expectations clear and communicate them effectively to pupils. Model good practice yourself and ensure that your classroom is a welcoming and safe place for pupils to learn.

All behaviour management specialists will tell you that when you address the class you should not shout over pupils. If you ask most pupils they want a teacher who can control the class yet impose themselves without appearing too strict or controlling. A fine balance needs to be met. So if you want the attention of the whole class then make clear the signal that indicates you expect them to focus on you; remember, silence is sometimes more powerful than speech. Give your signal (perhaps a countdown from three) and then wait. The silence will spread like a wave and then you can address the group (even if it takes some time to establish this at first, it is important to persevere). Confrontation creates negativity and can take up valuable learning time, which impacts on others, so avoid it where possible. In mathematics lessons we often require pupils to bring additional equipment and a cause of frustration is when they don't have it, as this interrupts the flow of the lesson. But ask yourself, is it really worth interrupting learning and creating a negative atmosphere because a pupil forgets a pencil, undoing all of your good work in establishing a positive classroom climate? We all forget things from time to time and for some of us there are greater reasons than others. Know the social circumstances of your pupils. Have an equipment tray and if pupils forget then quietly issue the forgotten item and make a note of it. You can issue consequences at the end of the lesson as you feel necessary. How you interact with pupils is extremely important.

If I asked you to make a list of things you see and hear in a positive classroom environment no doubt praise would feature towards the top of the list. Praise is an essential part of the teacher–learner relationship. Welcome answers from pupils, whether they are correct or not, and think carefully about how you respond to incorrect answers. For example, do you simply say 'No, that's not correct', or do you use positive language: 'Thank you, we're not quite there, would anyone like to contribute?' Pupils who volunteer answers when asked (particularly if you adopt a hands-down policy) need to be praised for participating. We learn from mistakes and so wrong answers are as welcome as right answers! If, on the other hand, a pupil offers an excellent solution equal consideration needs to be given to your response; for example, if a pupil surprises you with a good answer and you comment 'Well done, I wasn't expecting that from you', the subliminal message is that you have low expectations of them. Use praise through positive language choices.

Finally, don't be afraid of noise. As long as pupils aren't discussing their holiday plans or weekend activities and are focused on the mathematics then noise is good. It means pupils are actively discussing and therefore learning from one another. So often if teachers hear the footsteps of a senior team member walking down the corridor they hush the class. Don't. Welcome the noise and invite the individual in to hear the wonderful discussions taking place in your classroom. This is where pupils make mathematics meaningful to themselves. The only thing for you to be clear about with the class is that when you give the signal (perhaps a whistle or a countdown from three) you expect all eyes and ears to be on you.

Finally, the very best teachers have high expectations of their pupils and they continue to communicate these expectations. They know their pupils well and monitor their progress against success criteria. They ensure that feedback on work is timely and informative, and ensure that they emphasise the importance of good presentation and content. They ask higher-order questions and carefully shape their questions to probe learning and drive progress. All of this contributes to a positive environment that serves to motivate pupils and promotes a culture for learning.

Seating arrangements

How you seat the class is your choice. A seating plan is a good idea, as is mixing the style of desk arrangements to suit the activity. The desk arrangement immediately says something to pupils. What would you think if you were a pupil walking into a classroom with desks grouped together compared with individual desks facing the front? Most pupils feel safer with desks grouped together as this means they have their peers close to support them, compared to single-file desks that make them feel like they are walking into an examination environment. Desk arrangement is therefore important and different desk arrangements will suit different learning activities (of course, this depends on whether you are fortunate enough to have a room with enough space to allow for different desk arrangements). Seating in rows facing the front can often be associated with teacher delivery and tables grouped together with peer discussion.

Individual desks give the impression of an assessment and if you want pupils to work individually and independently then this is the best arrangement. A variation of this is to have desks in pairs all facing the front. This then allows more easily for paired activities. This type of desk arrangement does not actively promote discussion and if you adopt this style of seating then ensure that as you address the class you circulate to avoid those at the back participating less actively.

A horseshoe arrangement focuses pupils on a more central point. They can all see each other, which will actively encourage discussion among pupils by allowing maximum interaction between them. As a facilitator of learning this seating arrangement also provides you with direct easy access to each pupil, allowing you to see clearly what all pupils are doing at all times. To ensure all pupils have a clear view of the board or other central resources then fan the tails of the horseshoe out (more like a flat-bottomed V shape). You can sit yourself down at one leg to become part of the discussion activity; this shape is closest to the concept of circle time while at the same time allowing all pupils to have a line of sight on the board.

A café arrangement in which pupils are grouped in fours or sixes facing each other is useful for active discussion or group work. This arrangement does not necessarily work well where you need high levels of individual and independent work. Sometimes this style of desk arrangement can prove difficult for all pupils to see the board or other focal point and, in turn, it is difficult for you to see what all pupils are doing at all times. This type of arrangement is therefore best suited to group work or group activities.

Desk arrangements are important, but of equal importance is where you seat individual pupils. You probably know who not to sit together and the challenge is the best way to pair or group pupils. Do you seat pupils next to someone of the same ability or do you pair pupils in a support pairing so that a more able pupil can support a pupil who is less able? There is power in both arrangements and, in all honesty, it is probably better to keep seating plans dynamic. Have a standard seating plan (for the usual layout of your room) and then mix it up when you change the seating arrangements for different activities. If seating is dynamic and pupils are used to being moved they are less likely to offer resistance when asked to sit in a different seat next to someone new. Pupils can then be grouped in similar abilities, mixed abilities, learning-style preference, gender groups or random groups (where you pick names out of a hat). Varying the groups within which pupils work develops their social skills, team-working ability and their role within the team (which will vary according to the dynamics of the group).

Where do you position yourself in your classroom? Do you often stand in the same place? Try varying where you stand. Stand in different areas of the classroom, at the front, side or at the back. What do you notice? Changing where you stand gives you a different perspective on your classroom and the learners within it. Standing at the back and asking questions can be quite an eye-opening experience. Suddenly all the pupils wonder if you are watching them and the pupils at the back can no longer try to go unnoticed.

What do pupils hear when they enter your classroom? One technique is to play music as pupils enter and are completing the bell work activity. When you stop the music is when you expect all pupils to stop what they are doing and face the front ready for you to address the class. This is a simple technique and gives pupils a clear signal. What do you play? There are those who advocate the use of classical music, but I don't know many pupils who appreciate this era and so more upbeat modern music with a positive message is good to use. Select the tunes you play carefully and the volume you play them at and set your expectations clearly to pupils, i.e. when the music stops is when they stop working and face the front. Some teachers like to play relaxing music quietly when pupils are working on certain activities. Again, this is personal choice and it needs to suit the learners (some pupils will not like having music on in the background).

Classroom assistants

Do you honestly make the best use of classroom assistants in your classroom? Do you know whether a classroom assistant is going to be in your lesson? Do you know who it is? Do you know whether they are there to offer one-to-one support or work with a group of pupils? Chances are that at one time or another we can all answer 'no' to some or all of these questions.

First of all you should know who is coming into your classroom, when and the reason why. In most schools it is the role of the learning support department to provide you with this information. The next step is down to you. You need to arrange a regular time to meet with the teaching assistant who is working in your classroom. Share your lesson plan and discuss in advance of the lesson the learning that you expect to take place and the role you wish the teaching assistant to play. An important part of their role in your lesson is that they support the pupil or pupils they are working with and do not do the learning for them. This is an important distinction and some teaching assistants will end up doing the work for the pupil; the pupil then expects this and so will not develop in their own learning and will not make progress in mathematics. By liaising in advance of the lesson you will work to prevent this and create a more powerful and effective learning environment. If you require the teaching assistant to work with a particular group of pupils, then ensure that you work with the teaching assistant on how to facilitate learning rather than take over the learning or get too involved with the group.

Teaching assistants can provide valuable insight into the learning of the individual pupil they work closely with or on the groups they work regularly with. Equally, they can offer a different angle to your lesson. You may wish them to become involved by posing a problem they encountered in real life. You may, for example, ask them to bring in a till receipt. They can read out the prices of individual items and then ask pupils how much change they got from a £20 note, for example. Alternatively, they could tell pupils the amount of change they got and then ask them to work out the value of the missing item they purchased. Make it interesting and visual for pupils, so bring in a shopping bag with some items in it (children's plastic food items are great for this), pull them out one by one and show pupils the price (pre-label them). Pupils can note the price of each item and you can then pose the question of the missing price on the final item. This just makes it more interesting for pupils, rather than a list of numbers read to them (which becomes abstract) or a list of numbers on the board. It helps to engage them.

Continuing the shopping theme, they could tell pupils of a special offer in the supermarket. Is it better to buy packets of 80 teabags on three for two at £1.80 each or a large packet of 240 teabags at £3.75? They may bring in a train timetable and ask pupils to work out how they get from London to Birmingham, or two holiday brochures costing a similar holiday. It is important to remember that the teaching assistant is not a substitute teacher, but they do need to feel valued; if you have a teaching assistant in your classroom then work with them to support learning in the most effective way possible. No one can be expected to do the best at their job working blind. You wouldn't go blind into a classroom and neither should you expect that of a teaching assistant. They may not be a maths specialist and so will need your support in ensuring that they support the learning of the pupil in the correct mathematical way.

The outdoor learning environment

Mathematics is all around us. How do we engage our young pupils if we always sit in the same seats in the same classroom for every maths lesson? Take your classroom outside. Use the outdoor environment as an alternative learning space and an opportunity to use a resource that is different to using a worksheet or textbook.

This is not an excuse for 'it's hot Miss, please can we go outside and do our lesson?' (which we have all heard before).

This is about well-planned relevant learning opportunities that enhance the learning experience and engage young minds, allowing them to make connections between mathematics and real life. There are lots of outside learning opportunities and the key to making them successful is careful planning to ensure that the pupils are fully aware of what they need to achieve in a given time frame.

- Making and using clinometers to measure angles and use trigonometry to calculate the height of trees or buildings in the school grounds is an excellent way to make trigonometry more than just a set of problems on a worksheet. It gives pupils the opportunity to see how trigonometry can be used in real-life settings (albeit a little primitive with homemade clinometers). You can also engage in interesting discussions; for example, 'How do you use the information that you obtain?' 'Can you draw a sketch of the scenario and determine the measures we need to take?' 'How can we account for the height of the person using the clinometer in the calculation?' 'Why are all of our heights not the same for each building?' 'What variables are there?'

- Maths trails give pupils a lot of fun and if they are done well can be enriching activities. NRICH maths (http://nrich.maths.org) has some good ideas and examples of maths trails, with cards pre-prepared that you can edit and adapt. Maths trails are perhaps more popular with younger pupils, but are a good way of introducing outdoor maths in the earlier years and you can design them to an appropriate level of challenge.

- Observe symmetry in nature. Go on a walk in the school grounds (autumn is best for this) and ask pupils to find the most symmetrical leaf that they can. They can then take this leaf inside and test whether is it truly symmetrical. What properties would a symmetrical leaf have? How can you determine if something is symmetrical? Alternatively, they can collect ten different leaves from under the same tree (for example, if you wanted to find the mean and median length of an oak leaf in the school grounds) and use these to find the median leaf length and mean leaf length and compare the two averages. They can then form groups with teams that have collected leaves from under the same tree or from the same species and combine their results to find the new median and new mean leaf length from all, combining their original ten to create a larger sample. Is this a more accurate estimate? What factors influence the results? Are there any outliers? Which is the best average to use and why? Collecting statistics from the outdoor environment and using them in calculations is a way of encouraging pupils to engage with statistics in a real-life context. Indeed, the outdoor classroom is excellent for bringing data handling or statistics to life and increases the accessibility of mathematics for all learning styles.

- There are lots of different loci activities that can be done outside of the classroom to really embed the idea of path. Many pupils don't understand loci because of the word itself (it is not something they can relate to as it is not a word that is in common usage). Linking it with the concept of instructions and paths is a way of bringing loci to life. For example, place a cone on the floor and ask pupils to stand so that each pupil is two metres from the cone (they need to approximate the distance or use a two-metre length of rope). You can then link to the shape that this forms. Other ideas include giving pupils a piece of rope in teams to help them visualise the tethered goat problem, in which a goat is tied to a post with a three-metre length of rope and pupils have to shade or describe the region in which the goat is contained for grazing and therefore the loci of points. This can be extended to incorporate the corner of a building where the goat is tied to a corner and pupils have to describe the new area grazed by the goat (and then the loci of points).

There are lots of different outside learning opportunities and we should always explore the possibility of different ways of bringing mathematics alive for pupils. These add to and deepen their mathematical experiences and exposure and make them think in different contexts. The mathematics you take outdoors does not have to be complicated, but it does have to be carefully planned. The aim is to inspire and captivate young minds.

Summary

The classroom environment plays an important role in learning. Whether we are conscious of it or not, when we walk into a dull environment it has an impact on our mood, and the classroom is no exception. It is so much more than just the physical appearance.

Features key to creating a positive culture for learning through the classroom environment include:

- creating a positive image and never underestimating the impact of your own enthusiasm
- always having high expectations
- being aware of any 'habits' you may have as a teacher
- being consistent and addressing behaviour in a positive way
- creating dynamic classroom displays that form part of an active learning strategy
- changing seating arrangements to suit the activity and optimise learning
- liaising effectively with teaching assistants and involving them in the lesson
- using the outdoor environment to support and enhance learning.

CHAPTER 9

Pulling it all together

In this chapter we look in detail at developing lessons covering:

- expansion of two linear expressions to produce a quadratic expression
- indices
- ratio
- trigonometry.

Lots of different ideas for lessons are discussed in this book and we have looked in detail at how we can encourage mathematical independence and support pupils to develop key concepts without the direct teaching of factual methods. Now we can apply this to some sample lessons using the model: bell work, big question, starter activity, main activities, plenary activities and focus on the use of independent thinking, questioning, assessment of/for/as learning and differentiation.

A variety of different topics at different levels has been used to illustrate the ideas and you will know the ability level of your pupils and therefore the level at which you build, develop and pitch the activities. The aim is not to be prescriptive but to look at how you might pull together the ideas discussed in this book and start to develop a simple learning journey. The examples used are for discrete lessons; of course, many lessons are open-ended and roll into one another to allow pupils the opportunity to develop investigations or to work together on team projects. The lessons discussed here are simply to support developing lesson planning.

As you read through the individual lessons it is not necessarily about the activities used (these can be varied and designed to suit your own pupils and the type of lesson or learning that you want to create), but about how we introduce the concepts without directly teaching them, ensuring that as a teacher we at no point tell pupils a method but encourage them to develop methods independently and therefore we facilitate the learning. It is this that is perhaps most important.

Expanding two linear expressions to produce a quadratic expression

As you are greeting pupils at the classroom door there needs to be an initial bell work activity for pupils to engage with as soon as they take their seat. Remember, bell work can be any simple activity that reinforces numerical development. A simple settling bell work activity for this type of lesson is:

1) -3×-4
2) 8×-7
3) -12×11
4) 3×-3
5) 7×9

As simple as this activity is, it does actually serve a purpose. It gets pupils thinking about, recalling and using the rules for the multiplication of positive and negative integers. This doesn't need to be reviewed now as the starter activity can incorporate and therefore reinforce these facts. It is simply about switching pupils' minds to numeracy as soon as they enter the classroom (as they have probably come from an unrelated subject) and this basic lower-order cognitive skill of factual recall lends itself naturally to the numeracy skills that will be used during the lesson.

Once all of the pupils have arrived and you are ready to start the lesson, give your signal, count down from three, stop music playing or blow the whistle and introduce the Big Question. There are many different Big Questions to choose from for this lesson and a flavour is given in Figures 9.1 and 9.2. Remember, only one is needed and pupils should place their answer in a sealed envelope to be returned to at the end of the lesson as a measure of progress. Only one minute is given to this activity as we want immediate initial responses.

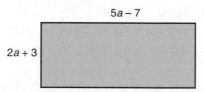

Figure 9.1 What is the area of the rectangle?

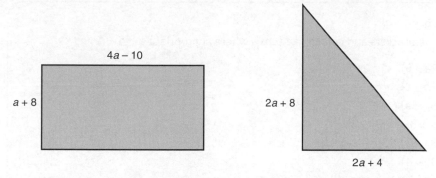

Figure 9.2 Oliver says the area of the triangle is bigger than the area of the rectangle. Do you agree? Justify your answer.

If you want to share learning outcomes at the beginning of your lesson then now is an appropriate time to show pupils the learning outcomes and grade-referenced criteria:

- Grade D: be able to multiply a single term over a bracket, e.g. $3(a + 2)$.

- Grade C: be able to expand and simplify the product of two simple linear brackets, e.g. $(x - 1)(x + 2)$.

- Grade B: be able to expand any linear expression, e.g. $(3x + 5)(2x + 3)$.

- Grade B/A: be able to expand brackets such as $(a - p)(2p + q)$ and extend to problem solving.

You may choose not to do this and ask pupils to identify the key learning outcomes as part of the self-reflection and review exercise towards the end of the lesson (I think this is probably the best approach). In any case, the learning outcomes show a sequence in techniques.

The lesson begins with the starter activity and there are lots of different starter activities that link nicely and initiate the learning for this topic. Below we discuss a few ideas.

Starter activities that benchmark pupils and assess prior knowledge include those where a single term is multiplied over a bracket and/or questions that involve collecting like terms. These can be done individually in books, on mini-whiteboards, or iPads or other tablet devices. Mini-whiteboards, or tablets used in a similar fashion, probably offer the best visual feedback and allow you to assess the whole class (including the method that they have used). Carefully select each of the questions used in the starter activity, ensuring that each has a specific learning purpose or theme that you can discuss with the class on review.

Example 9.1
Expand the brackets and collect like terms where appropriate.

1) $-3(2a - 6)$
2) $-4(2b - 2)$
3) $-3(8 - 5a)$
4) $6(2y + 3) - 4(2y - 8)$
5) $-3(3 - 8y) - 5(2 - 2y)$
6) $2y(3y - 4)$

During the review the questions you ask are important. Remember to adopt a 'hands-down' policy and bounce questions around the classroom in the basketball style discussed in Chapter 5.

For example, a pupil has given the correct answer to question (1) of Example 9.1 of $-6a + 18$. You then further probe this by asking another pupil 'Fred, do you agree?' Following Fred's agreement or disagreement you can then ask him to explain why $-3(2a - 6)$ gives us $-6a + 18$. This can then bounce to a different pupil to remind us of the rules of multiplying positive and negative integers. This line of questioning can be continued with each of the starter activity questions, summarising the learning purpose of each question and keeping pupils on their toes. Following the starter activity pupils can then assess their prior knowledge with marks out of the given total. They can then indicate areas with which they had difficulty. This can be used to focus support during the lesson.

It is important to recap any pertinent information resulting from the starter activity. Therefore ask pupils to write in a 'thought bubble' the rules for multiplying positive and negative integers, along with some examples. There are lots of different variations of this starter activity as you can imagine. It works very well as a pair-matching activity where pupils work individually or in pairs to match the question with the solution. What is important is that this activity should take no longer than seven minutes in total (including review) and so you must maintain a good pace.

A different starter activity is finding the area of rectangles. This can be used as a theme to encourage pupils to recall and think about the formula for the area of rectangles. Examples are shown in Figure 9.3.

In the review it is important to establish that pupils are comfortable with the concept of length multiplied by width to determine the area of the rectangle in each case. Other alternatives involve making a connection with number grids, such as in Example 9.2.

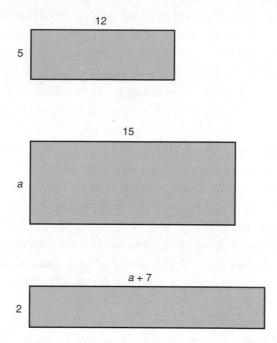

Figure 9.3 Find the area of the rectangles.

Example 9.2

If we write 27 as 20 + 7, then how can we write 13 (i.e. 10 + 3)? Complete the grid multiplication shown in Table 9.1.

Table 9.1 Complete the multiplication grid.

x	20	7
10		
3		

Given that 27 = 30 − 3 and 13 = 10 + 3, complete the number grid 30 − 3 × 10 + 3 shown in Table 9.2.

Table 9.2 Complete the multiplication grid.

x	30	−3
10		
3		

1) Why are the two answers the same?
2) Can you give a further example which will give the answer of 351?

Discussions of Example 9.2 should revolve around the idea of breaking a number into components $x + y$ that can be linked to grid multiplication in algebra. Remember, making connections in mathematics is how we build mathematical learners. This starter activity encourages connections in learning and really supports the underlying conceptual development. It can be extended further later in the main activity, replacing 10 with x, leading to, for example, $(3x - 3)$ $(x + 3)$.

Assessment and discussion of this activity need to focus on the relationship between number and breaking a number into its components.

Remember, during the review of the starter activity, addressing misconceptions and steering the learning towards the key concepts upon which the learning will be developed are key.

We then progress to learning in the main, where we develop the main mathematical concept. In this case it is encouraging pupils to apply their mathematical knowledge to develop a method for multiplying two linear expressions, such as $(a + 3)(a + 7)$.

Now is the time to pose a think, pair, share question. Again, there are many different variations on this and we discuss below a few of the potential applications.

Figure 9.4 follows from the area starter and Figure 9.5 follows from the grid multiplication starter.

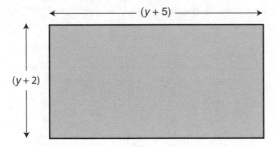

Figure 9.4 Development of the area starter activity.

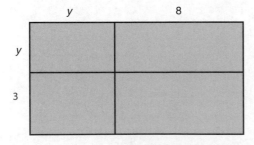

Figure 9.5 Development of the grid multiplication starter activity.

We use Figure 9.4 to ask pupils if they have any ideas on how to determine the area of the rectangle. We give them one minute to think about it and one minute to discuss their response in pairs. Using a hands-down policy, direct the questioning to ask a pupil or pair their thoughts. Probe this idea further with questioning and use the basketball approach.

- 'What concept are we using?'
- 'How do we know?'
- 'Can we break the "length" and "width" into component parts?'

Then ask pupils to calculate the area of the rectangle or complete the sum. Focus discussions on the correct multiplication of terms and correctly collecting like terms.

We use Figure 9.5 in a similar way, but ask pupils if they can break $y + 8$ into components and $y + 3$ into components to complete a multiplication grid.

Once the sharing process is complete ask pupils to work in pairs to determine an answer to the problem and to write in an 'ideas bubble' their thought process. The whole-class discussion can then focus on discussing the different ideas bubbles and developing a method.

Next are a few quick-fire questions to ensure that pupils can use their method to complete simple questions, such as $(b + 4)(b + 2)$. Whiteboards or iPads are good for this as you can instantly see whether pupils have correctly answered the question or not. If you have iPads and Apple TV you can link to individual iPads and allow the whole class to see different pupil responses for discussion purposes. Follow with a question such as $(a - 3)(a + 2)$, focusing on multiplication of positive and negative integers and correctly collecting like terms.

A quick pair-matching exercise is useful here to allow pupils time to consolidate their learning so far. They can complete this in pairs and it can be short (two minutes), and then the answers can simply be displayed on the board and pupils can self-mark. Alternatively, if you have an interactive whiteboard facility then you can display the pair-matching cards and pupils can come to the board and 'drag and drop' the correct match. Discussion is only really needed if pupils have got answers incorrect (this is because the discussion for learning was completed earlier) or to reinforce important mathematical points as necessary.

Next we extend the concept further and introduce coefficients of the unknown that are greater than one, for example $(2y + 1)(3y + 4)$.

This is where pupil understanding is really tested. Allow pupils time to work on this as a pair. Circulate and listen to the discussions, noting any themes that warrant further discussion as a class. These can then be discussed during the whole-class review. Alternatively set pupils into small groups of four and give each group a different question to work on (two or three minutes only), elect a spokesperson and in the whole-class review they can then present their solution to the rest of the class. A further alternative to this is to ask teams to write their answers onto large A3 sheets of paper (A3 sugar paper and a variety of coloured marker pens are useful for this). Solutions can then be passed to another team for comments and then on to a third team for further feedback. You can circulate at this point and cast an eye over the answers. Discussion can be developed from this.

Common misconceptions at this stage include $5y^2 + 11y + 4$. That is, pupils have added the coefficients of y rather than multiplied. If you see this in a response ensure that it is unpicked and worked through as a class.

Once this is complete and you are happy with the discussions add a mini-assessment with a few quick-fire questions involving multiplying expressions in two brackets.

Ask pupils to self-mark and rate (or RAG rate) their performance. This, along with your observations, will be used to support pupils in the self-selection of the differentiated materials. Here I suggest three different worksheet-based activities (spend no longer than ten or fifteen minutes on these, as you judge to be appropriate). Pupils are to self-select questions from the worksheets that they choose, ensuring that they all answer the applied question on their respective worksheet (give a two-minute warning to them so that they know when to move on to this question). The idea is not for pupils to continue to repeat similar question after question but to allow pupils to practice similar questions until they are confident and then to progress to the applied questions. Figures 9.6–9.8 show worksheets that offer support from the less able to the more able respectively.

For the following questions multiply out the bracket (show your working)

1   $3(a + 4)$
2   $4(2y - 5)$
3   $-6(-2 - 3y)$
4   $8(4 - 7y)$

For the following questions multiply out the brackets (show all working)

5   $(a + 4)(a + 3)$
6   $(b + 5)(b - 3)$
7   $(a - 8)(a - 2)$
8   $(c - 7)(c - 8)$
9   $(y + 6)(y - 9)$
10 $(a + 3)(a - 12)$
11 $(v + 2)(3 - v)$
12 $(b + 5)(b - 8)$
13 $(g - 6)(g + 2)$
14 $(h + 6)(h - 7)$
15 $(9 - f)(f - 2)$
16 $(a + 12)(a - 12)$

Multiply out the brackets (show all working)

17 $(2a + 4)(a + 2)$
18 $(2f - 3)(f - 6)$
19 $(p + 1)(3p - 1)$
20 $(3a + 7)(4a + 2)$
21 $(5b - 1)(6b - 5)$
22 $(a + 4)^2$
23 $(2p - 1)(2p + 1)$
24 $(8m - 3)(5 - 2m)$

25 A farmer has a rectangular field of length $(a + 3)$ and width $(a + 2)$.

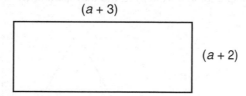

$(a + 3)$

$(a + 2)$

a   How do you work out the area of a rectangle?
b   Write an expression for the area of the rectangle
c   Expand any brackets

Figure 9.6 Expanding two brackets to produce a quadratic expression.

For the following questions expand the brackets using either method (show all working)

1 $(a + 4)(a + 3)$
2 $(b + 5)(b - 3)$
3 $(a - 8)(a - 2)$
4 $(c - 7)(c - 8)$
5 $(y + 6)(y - 9)$
6 $(2a + 4)(3a + 2)$
7 $(2f - 3)(f - 6)$
8 $(3p + 1)(3p - 1)$
9 $(3a - 7)(10a - 12)$
10 $(5b - 1)(6b + 9)$

Multiply out the brackets and then simplify your expressions where possible

11 $(m + n)(3n - m)$
12 $(a + 4)^2$
13 $(2p + 1)(3p + 2) - 4p + 1$
14 $(a - 2)^2 - 2a + 3$
15 $(2b - 5)^2$
16 $(2p + 3a)(2p - 3a) + 9a^2$

17 For the rectangle

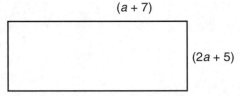

a   Write an expression for the area (expand any brackets)
b   Write an expression for the perimeter (simplify where possible)

18 Write an expression for the area the triangle shown below (expand any brackets)

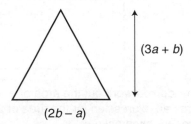

Figure 9.7 Expanding two brackets to produce a quadratic expression.

For the following questions multiply out the brackets (show all working)

1 $(a + 4)(a + 3)$
2 $(b + 5)(b - 3)$
3 $(a - 8)(a - 2)$
4 $(c - 7)(c - 8)$
5 $(y + 6)(y - 9)$
6 $(2a + 4)(3a + 2)$
7 $(2f - 3)(f - 6)$
8 $(3p + 1)(3p - 1)$

In the following questions multiply out the brackets and then simplify your expressions where possible

9 $(2m + n)(3n - m)$
10 $(3a + 4)^2$
11 $(2p - 7)(3p - 5) - 4p + 1$
12 $(a - 2)^2 - 2a + 3$
13 $(2b - 5)^2$
14 $(2p + 3a)(2p - 3a) + 9a^2$

17 For the rectangle (not drawn to scale)

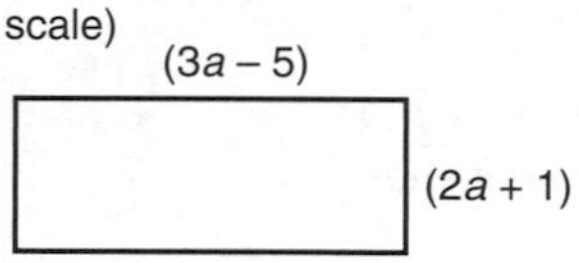

$(3a - 5)$

$(2a + 1)$

a Write an expression for the area (expand any brackets)
b Write an expression for the perimeter
c If the perimeter is 92 cm what is the length of the longest side?
d What is the area of the rectangle?

18 A circle has radius $(2a + 4)$. Write an expression in terms of pi for the area of the circle. Expand any brackets.

19 By expanding both sides or otherwise show that:
$$(m^2 + 1)(n^2 + 1) = (m + n)^2 + (mn - 1)^2$$

Figure 9.8 Expanding two brackets to produce a quadratic expression.

Once the time allotted for this activity is over (remember to stress quality over quantity of answers), allow pupils a few minutes to self-mark their work (or peer-mark at this point). They also need to set themselves learning targets from the activity and may use the grade criteria given at the beginning to review their progress towards the learning outcomes (if you choose to use grade criteria).

As the learning journey moves to the end of the lesson, we reach the final assessment activity. It is important to always make time for the final assessment activity (dedicate approximately ten minutes at the end of a one-hour lesson) to allow you to make a final assessment of the learning.

Figure 9.9 show examples of plenary questions that can be used to determine if progress has been made during the lesson. I suggest using mini-whiteboards or iPads for this phase as it allows you to instantly review responses and assess the performance of all of the pupils in the class simultaneously. At this stage ensure questioning develops their metacognition – in other words that they think about thinking.

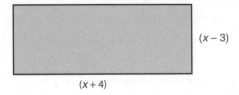

$(x - 3)$

$(x + 4)$

The area of the rectangle is $78\,cm^2$.

a   Use this information to write down an equation in terms of x.

b   Show that your equation in part can be written as

$$x^2 + x - 90 = 0$$

Figure 9.9 An example of a plenary question.

Or set questions of the style, 'If the answer is $x^2 + 7x + 10$ then what two brackets were multiplied together $(x + ?)(x + ?)$?' This really probes understanding and encourages pupils to properly think about the underlying concept and the process they have actually used.

Finally, return to the Big Question. Put the Big Question back on the interactive whiteboard, or whichever medium you used to display it initially, and ask pupils to retry the question. They can then open their envelopes and compare their response at the start of the lesson to that at the end. Have they made progress? How do they know? Can they identify the mistakes in their initial response? If pupils stick the initial and final response into their books then you can see the progress that they have made in their learning. But remember the most important role of the Big Question is that it leaves pupils with a sense of success and completion as they leave your lesson. In being able to complete the Big Question at the end of the lesson they have shown themselves that they have made progress and, more importantly, they can articulate what that progress is.

As pupils leave the classroom put the bell work questions back up and ask individual pupils for a response as they leave. In this lesson we haven't told or taught pupils any methods; instead, they have developed the concepts themselves through a series of carefully guided activities. This ensures that they have thought about the underlying processes, which promotes independence in their thinking. One further point to note is that as a teacher you haven't done much talking, adding to the lesson only to summarise or to place emphasis on key mathematical concepts.

Let us summarise this lesson with some indicative timings and notes. Pace is important, but not at the detriment of learning, so flexibility is important; the lesson should be adapted, if appropriate, with activities included or omitted to suit your learners and the pace of learning that secures optimum success. The lesson is based on a 60 minute lesson. We will use the rectangle method as an example. The writing is in note form, intended to support lesson planning and timings are intended for guidance only (timings depend on the abilities and progress of the learners and should be adjusted, as appropriate; the key is to avoid drift).

A summary of the lesson is given in brief:

Bell work (two minutes): numeracy from the outset

- As pupils arrive engage them with the bell work activity which promotes numerical skills to be used in the lesson. Not to be reviewed at this stage.

Starter activity: assessment of prior knowledge

- Pupils to complete the Big Question individually (one minute only) and to seal in an envelope for later reference.
- Six quick-fire starter questions that will assess prior knowledge. To be completed individually in books (five minutes) or on mini-whiteboards.
- Review questions as a whole class using probing questions (adopt a hands down policy); pupils to self-mark and self-assess with a show of hands for marks out of six (three minutes).

Learning in the main: cycle of concept development, mini-assessments, meta-cognition and reviews

- Pose the rectangle problem. Use the cognitive rehearsal strategy: think, pair, share (four minutes).
- During the sharing phase use higher-order questioning to probe further and develop a method for finding the area of the rectangle and thus multiplying two brackets, e.g. $(y + 3)(y + 8)$ (five minutes).
- Pose two further problems for pupils to complete in pairs (four minutes).
- Review (two minutes).
- Discuss the correct mathematical language (one minute).
- Pose two different questions to be completed individually (four minutes).
- Pupils to self-assess and use to support self-selection of the worksheets (one minute).
- Pupils to self-select a worksheet from a choice of three (ten minutes). Circulate, observe and discuss with individuals. Provide a two-minute warning for pupils to move to the applied question.

- Place answers on board – peer assess (three minutes).
- Highlight any misconceptions or any key points or any questions that are good discussion points (five minutes).

Final assessment activity and final review (ten minutes): How have we done? How do we know?

- As a whole class decide on what the learning outcomes for the lesson were.
- Introduce the formal success criteria (graded if you feel appropriate).
- Pose the final plenary questions (mini-whiteboards to allow whole-class assessment).
- Return to the Big Question: do the answers differ now to the initial response? What have they learned during the lesson and how do they know?

Indices

In this lesson we focus on developing the rules for the multiplication and division of numbers written in index form. The most important point to note as you read through this example lesson is that at no point are pupils told the rules. They develop and test the rule independently, which makes the learning experience richer and much more powerful. The focus is on learning and not on teaching.

A good bell work activity for this lesson is the addition and subtraction of positive and negative integers, which encourages pupils to think about directed numbers. For example:

1) $-3 - 5$
2) $2 - -4$
3) $-18 + -3$
4) $-9 - 8$
5) $-12 + 5$

The Big Question can be an application of indices where pupils are asked to use given facts to deduce the answer to a calculation. They should only be given one minute to answer this, with answers being sealed in an envelope:

'Given $7^5 = 16,807$ and $7^8 = 5,764,801$, calculate $(7 \times 5,764,801)/16,807$ in less than one minute without using a calculator.'

A simple starter activity can be:

If $3^4 = 3 \times 3 \times 3 \times 3$

Then simplify:

1) $5 \times 5 \times 5 \times 5 \times 5$

2) $6 \times 6 \times 6$

3) $4 \times 4 \times 4 \times 4 \times 4 \times 4 \times 4 \times 4$

Expand:

4) 4^5

5) $3^2 \times 3^4$

Now simplify your answer in the form 3^n.

This can be assessed and discussed. Recap the notation and vocabulary, i.e. base and index (indices) and power.

Next is to pose a problem building on the last question in the starter activity, such as $3^4 \times 3^5$, and ask pupils to expand and simplify. This works as a nice group activity. Give pupils a few to complete as a group. Can they come up with a general rule?

As a class develop the concept of the addition of the indices when multiplying. Pose the question of $4^2 \times 5^4$. Does the same rule apply? Why not? So what must be the same in order for the rule to work?

Ask pupils in their groups to summarise the method in a thought bubble. You may want them to formalise this in their workbooks.

Now introduce division. Ask pupils in advance if they have any ideas. If a pupil comes up with the concept of subtraction then suggest the hypothesis and ask the class to test it. Summarise the findings as before through pupil-led discussion.

Assess the learning with a mixture of simple questions such as:

1) $6^4 \times 6^{10}$

2) $6^3 \times 6^{25}$

3) $4^7 \div 4^3$

4) $a^{20} \div a^4$

Ask pupils to peer assess, focusing on ensuring that the working step is shown, e.g. $5^2 \times 5^3 = 5^{(2+3)} = 5^5$.

Further challenges involving combined use of the rules can be posed to pupils individually, in pairs or in groups, e.g. $(5^{12} \times 5^3)/(5^7 \times 5^4)$. Discussions can evolve around whether the order of operations matters.

As the lesson develops further you can introduce problems, such as $5a^2 \times 3a^4$. Ask pupils in groups to investigate the answer. Do a similar problem involving division. Encourage pupils to think of $5a^2 \times 3a^4 = 5 \times a^2 \times 3 \times a^4$.

Negative indices can be introduced simply by using the concepts already developed. For example, pose the problem a^2 divided by a^4. Encourage pupils to use the rule for division of numbers in index form to yield a^{-2} and then to expand the top and bottom line of the expression to yield $1/a^2$, leading to the equivalence of $a^{-2} = 1/a^2$. Pupils can be asked to demonstrate this with further examples.

Pulling it all together

A mini-assessment is useful at this point to determine which main learning activity pupils should select.

An example of a mini-assessment is:

1) $5a^7 \times 5a^{-3}$
2) $4b^5 \times 3b^{-5}$
3) $21p^4 \div 3p^8$
4) $(5m^2 \times 4m^9)/(2m^7 \times m^8)$

The pace of this lesson is important and should drive the learning. Remember, emphasis is on learning, not teaching.

The main activity can be varied. If you choose to use a worksheet then Figure 9.10 shows an example in which pupils can self-select or alternatively differentiated worksheets can be developed styled on this example. These should last approximately 15 minutes and offer pupils sufficient thinking time. Pupils can self-assess, or there is an opportunity for peer review. Pupils should use these results and the results of the mini-assessments during the lesson to set learning targets.

$$a^n \times a^m = a^{n+m}$$
$$b^n \div b^m = b^{n-m}$$

$$a^{-n} = \frac{1}{a^n}$$

A Simplify each of the following

1 $x^2 \times x^5$	2 $b^5 \times b^2$	3 $g^5 \times g^{-2}$	4 $m^{12} \times m^{-3}$
5 $5^3 \times 5^7$	6 $y^{10} \times y^{12}$	7 $h^{-2} \times h^7$	8 $c^4 \times c^{-4}$
9 $5m^3 \times 3m^2$	10 $4y^7 \times 9y^{12}$	11 $am^3 \times bm^5$	

B Simplify each of the following

1 $x^{10} \div x^5$	2 $4^{12} \div 4^7$	3 $c^5 \div c^2$	4 $y^{15} \div y^{12}$
5 $g^5 \div g^{-2}$	6 $h^{-2} \div h^7$	7 $m^{12} \div m^{-3}$	8 $d^5 \div d^{-5}$
9 $15m^5 \div 3m^2$	10 $28y^9 \div 4y^3$	11 $55m^3 \div 11m^5$	

C Write each of the following using a negative power

1 $\dfrac{1}{5}$	2 $\dfrac{1}{12}$	3 $\dfrac{1}{a}$	4 $\dfrac{1}{b^2}$
5 $\dfrac{1}{c^3}$	6 $\dfrac{1}{d^7}$	7 $\dfrac{5}{x^4}$	8 $\dfrac{A}{m^3}$

D Simplify each of the following

1 $4m^{12} \times 3m^3 \times 2m^2$	2 $15m^5 \div 3m^2 \times 2m^3$
3 $3b^{12} \times 2b^{-3} \times 4b^2$	4 $20m^4 \div 4m^3 \times 2m^{-3}$

E Find some values of y which meet each of the following conditions
1 y^2 is always larger than y
2 y^2 is always smaller than y
3 y^2 is equal to y

Figure 9.10 An example of a worksheet for indices.

If you wish to create a more active learning environment (rather than using a worksheet) then there is the opportunity for different work stations where pupils can use the concepts developed during the lesson to contribute solutions to problems that involve the application of indices. For exam groups this may be different past examination questions. Alternatively, you may use this time for groups to produce a pictorial summary or to spot misconceptions in answers to problems. There are lots of alternatives for the main activity; the importance is not, perhaps, the activity itself but that it contributes to the learning journey and enables pupils to make mathematical progress, developing their thinking as they work.

The final assessment activity or plenary can again take different forms. You may wish to have a true or false quiz or a multiple response quiz. If you have one, electronic voting systems are very good to use. Alternatively, you may wish to use simple questions that visibly verify through the use of mini-whiteboards whether pupils can approach applied questions (be wary that this is not just more of the same), such as 'What is the value of b in $48 \times 56 = 3 \times 7 \times 2b$?' or to place an answer, e.g. 3^7, and ask pupils what the question was (this always gives nicely differentiated responses). Whatever activity you choose it should allow you to make a final assessment of the whole class. If a more complicated Big Question was used then you may choose to dedicate the final assessment opportunity to a thorough discussion and create a more open-ended plenary, which perhaps can lead to a home-learning investigation. In any case, refer back to the Big Question and give pupils the opportunity to solve it. Can they apply their newly acquired knowledge? How has what they have learned during the lesson helped them in answering the Big Question more thoroughly? Have they made progress in their learning? How do they know?

Finally, as pupils leave the classroom answer the bell work in reverse.

Dividing in a given ratio

Ratio is a wonderful opportunity to bring mathematics alive for pupils. A simple starter is to ask pupils in teams of four to complete equivalent ratios and write down as many equivalent ratios as possible in one minute. An example is shown in Figure 9.11.

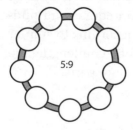

Figure 9.11 Equivalent ratios.

Pupils can then swap with another team who will mark their answers. They will set their own marking criteria and discussion may surround that; for example, given the ratio 5:4 pupils often perceive that 35:28 is a better answer than 50:40. You can ask the teams who mark the work to highlight answers that they 'like', offering reasons. They can also be asked to highlight any errors.

This moves to the main activity, which involves dividing a quantity into a given ratio. A nice activity to start pupils thinking is to have some money on tables (Monopoly money is good for this). Teams of four are then asked to complete a few questions.

The first may be, 'Divide £100 into five equal piles. How much money is in each pile?'

Alternatively, you may start with a problem such as '£100 is shared into bags containing equal amounts of money such that Anne gets one bag and Helen gets four bags. Between them Anne and Helen have all of the money. How much money does Helen get? How much money does Helen have compared with Anne? What is the ratio of Anne's money to Helen's? How else could the question have been written?'

Pupils can then be asked to apply to the problem, 'This time £100 is shared between Anne and Helen in the ratio 2:3. How much money does Helen get?'

Using counters or money as a prompt supports kinaesthetic learners, but also helps pupils to visualise the problem. Pupils need sufficient time to think about this problem.

Discussion can be based around how we know, for example, that Anne gets two parts in the second example and not three parts. The importance is in ensuring that pupils develop the method themselves and that we simply facilitate the process and do not tell them the method (which would then make the process simply rote learning).

Once a method has been established you can give pupils a series of problems to work on. They can produce a podcast or a poster or any medium of their choice to demonstrate the method. Give each team a minute to decide on the medium they are going to use and then five minutes to produce their final product.

A nice activity is to use recipes (an example worksheet is shown in Figure 9.12) and to ask each team to choose a starter, main course and pudding and to then solve the problems. If teams are grouped according to similar ability profiles then the menus can be different for each team, challenging the more able with, for example, dividing a ratio into three or more parts.

Restaurant Blanc

Starter

Prawn Cocktail
2 parts prawn to 5 parts salad to 3 parts butter makes prawn cocktail.
The total weight is 210g.

Find the weight of

    a   prawns   b   salad   c   butter

Nut Crunch
2 parts nuts to 3 parts bread crumbs to 1 part egg makes nut crunch.
The total weight is 240g.

Find the weight of

    a   nuts   b   bread crumbs   c   egg

Vegetable Soup
2 parts vegetables to 3 parts stock to 4 parts water makes vegetable soup.
The total weight is 270g.

Find the weight of

    a   vegetables   b   stock   c   water

Main

Cottage Pie
1 part beef to 3 parts potato to 5 parts carrots makes cottage pie.
The total weight is 630g.

Find the weight of

    a   beef   b   potato   c   carrots

Chicken Salad
3 parts salad to 2 parts chicken to 1 part croutons makes chicken salad.
The total weight is 420g.

Find the weight of

    a   chicken   b   salad   c   croutons

Desserts

Chocolate Ice
4 parts chocolate to 5 parts cream to 1 part sugar makes chocolate ice.
The total weight is 180g.

Find the weight of

    a   chocolate   b   cream   c   sugar

Lemon Sorbet
1 part lemon to 2 parts sugar makes lemon sorbet.
The total weight is 120g.

Find the weight of

    a   lemon   b   sugar

Figure 9.12 An example of using a menu to divide quantities into a given ratio.

The plenary may pose questions in reverse, such as, 'If May receives £22, Lily receives £66 and Tulip receives £12, how much money was shared and in what ratio (give your answer in its simplest form)?'

The key to developing these lessons is to allow pupils sufficient thinking time, but to ensure that you are able to judge when they have had just enough time or when to stop and intervene. It is important to introduce the concept in a way that engages them and allows them to think for themselves, in other words removing the taught factor.

Trigonometry

Many pupils are simply told that the sine of an angle is equal to the length of the opposite side divided by the length of the hypotenuse.

But how many of them actually understand what that means? How many actually link this to the ratio of the two sides?

A nice Big Question is, 'Amy says that it is impossible to find the length of the missing side without measuring it with a ruler, given the information in Figure 9.13. Do you agree or disagree?'

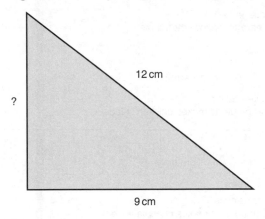

Figure 9.13 Can you find the missing side in this right-angled triangle?

To start the lesson off ask pupils to draw a large right-angled triangle (they can use the squares in their book to ensure that the triangle is an accurate right angle, or you may choose to provide some large right-angled triangles that you have pre-drawn on a square grid, or you can use a computer program if you have access to a computer suite or tablets). Ask pupils to measure the angle and then each side of the triangle to complete Table 9.3.

Table 9.3 A table for recording the results of measuring the right-angled triangle (d.p., decimal places).

Angle (°)	Opposite (cm)	Adjacent (cm)	Hypotenuse (cm)	Opposite/ hypotenuse (to 3 d.p.)	Adjacent/ hypotenuse (to 3 d.p.)	Opposite/ adjacent (to 3 d.p.)

Then ask pupils to make the triangle smaller by drawing a line parallel to the opposite side (as shown in Figure 9.14). Pupils measure the sides of the newly formed triangle and repeat this process a few times. Hopefully all the pupils have triangles with different angles but all deduce that the ratio of the sides is the same given a fixed angle. Accuracy of measurements may need to be discussed here (which is why computer programs have the advantage).

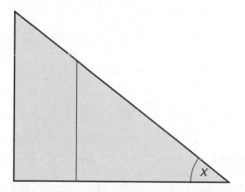

Figure 9.14 Creating a new triangle within the original one.

Now challenge their thinking further and ask pupils to draw a new triangle inside their large triangle and to only measure one side; for example, the hypotenuse. Ask them to try to work out the length of the opposite side using the information in their tables. Pupils can then check their answers by measuring the opposite side. They can discuss what they have done in pairs or you may wish to make this a paired activity. This can be repeated for another side.

It is important at some point in the process to make reference to the names given to the different ratios (e.g. sine, cosine and tangent) and their respective definitions. Pupils can be asked to use their calculators to find the value of sine 30°, for example, and then to discuss what this means (e.g. for a triangle with an angle of 30° the length of the opposite side divided by the length of the hypotenuse will always be 0.5). Ensuring that pupils can correctly use their calculator is important here.

A question can then be posed for a triangle with an angle of 30° with the opposite side known but the hypotenuse unknown. The ratio of the two sides can be used to find the missing side.

Developing trigonometry in this way allows pupils to think about what the respective ratios actually mean and goes some way to reducing the perceived complexity of trigonometry and to unravelling the mystery often associated with it. The only memory element comes in pupils remembering the definition of each ratio.

Once you have established this understanding, pose a problem to the class such as that in Figure 9.15. This can be made more interesting by perhaps making it a question involving finding the height of a building.

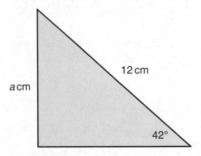

Figure 9.15 An example of a mini-assessment question.

Pupils can work in groups to support their understanding. They must first label the missing side and decide on what information they already know and then discuss how trigonometry can be used to solve this problem. Other problems can be posed to pupils individually and can then be used as a mini-assessment to determine selection of the individual learning activity. Alternatively, pupils can work in groups rotating to different work stations tackling different problems.

The plenary may include application of trigonometry questions such as those in Figures 9.16 and 9.17.

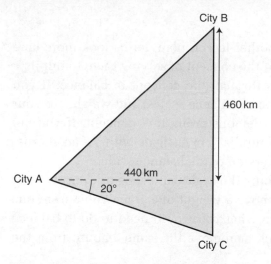

Figure 9.16 Find the distance from City B to City C.

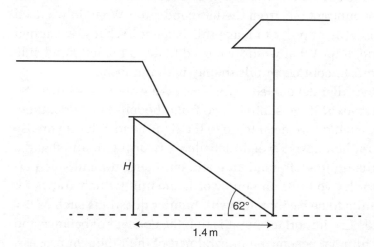

Figure 9.17 An architect has left his drawing incomplete; find the height of the wall marked *H*.

Ultimately, the aim of this lesson is to introduce trigonometry through the pupils themselves. In other words, we are not teaching them a method that they must rote learn and apply, but encouraging independence through investigation. In a subsequent lesson make clinometers and use the outside learning space to reinforce trigonometry in a real-life scenario, as discussed in Chapter 8.

Solving equations

Without going into detail through another lesson plan, let us look more here about how to introduce equations and the concept of solving them to pupils.

I really like introducing equations through the concept of balance. If you have any old laboratory scales (equal-arm balance scales) and weights in your school then these are wonderful for demonstrating this concept. If you are lucky you will have a set for groups of pupils to investigate with. As an alternative, seek an interactive whiteboard version of the balance scale.

First, demonstrate to pupils balancing the scales and then ask pupils what they think will happen when you remove a weight of a given value from one side. Test their suggestions. Ask them what you would need to do to balance the scales (either add the weight back or remove the same amount from the other side of the pivot).

Develop this to the idea of a basic sum, such as $2 + 3 = 5$.

What happens if we subtract one from the left-hand side? What do we need to do to the right-hand side in order to make this balance? What if we added seven to the right-hand side? What would we need to do to the left-hand side to balance the equation? Encourage pupils to play with numbers.

The concept can be further developed to $x + 2 = 7$. We want x on its own. So what do we need to remove? If we subtract two from the left-hand side, then, using our knowledge, what do we need to do to the right-hand side? If you use the balance scales here then have a weight labelled x (worth five units) and a weight worth two units on the left-hand side and on the right-hand side perhaps three weights worth two units and one worth one unit (which allows for a weight worth two units to be easily removed). Similar questions such as $9 = 5 + x$ can be discussed. The important point is that the concept of balance and the relationship with number become an integral part of their thought process.

We now progress to situations such as $5a = 10$. Ask pupils what $5a$ means, e.g. $5 \times a$ or 5 lots of a. Ask pupils how we might work out the value of a. Most will automatically spot by inspection that $a = 2$. Ask pupils what mathematical process could lead to an answer of two and how they would calculate this if the numbers were not so simple. Can they relate this to any word problems? Remember to discuss the important of checking answers by substitution.

This can be developed to $5a + 4 = 14$ and to beginning to really understand the notion of balance in mathematics and how it is used to solve equations. Getting pupils used to manipulating numbers early in their mathematical careers helps in their mathematical confidence.

Summary

When planning for learning think first about the learning outcomes that you want pupils to achieve. Determine a suitable benchmark from which to start and then plan a sequence of activities that will introduce and develop the concept. Always be conscious of the level of input that you have and aim to achieve a fine balance between this and independent learning.

Planning for learning should answer the following questions:

- What outcomes do I want pupils to achieve?
- What are the success criteria?
- Have I set a challenging Big Question?
- Have I benchmarked the learning?
- Have I chosen an activity or a variety of activities that will develop independent thinking?
- Have I used active learning strategies and effectively sequenced activities?
- Am I aware of the pace and timings of each activity?
- Have I differentiated to ensure activities meet the needs of and challenge all learners?
- Have I thought about higher-order questions?
- Have I used assessment for learning strategies?
- Have I encouraged self-selection?
- Have I used a variety of individual, paired or group activities?
- Have I included a review?
- Do pupils know whether they have made progress?
- Have I included a challenging plenary?
- Have I returned to the Big Question?

If you can answer all of these questions then you will be on your way to planning for outstanding learning.

Conclusion

The aim of this book is to provide you with lots of different ideas and activities to support you in becoming an outstanding teacher in your everyday practice. It takes time to incorporate these ideas seamlessly into your lessons and for pupils to become used to more independent ways of working, so work on developing a few key themes first and then add to your portfolio. You can't do everything at once. You will find what works best for you and remember the same things may not work well for every class or for every teacher. That's why personalising your approach is so important and is what leads to outstanding practice in teaching and learning.

One of the key features to developing as a teacher is to observe others and not just other maths teachers. That's how we learn. Sharing good practice is how the very best teachers continue to achieve outstanding, they learn from others and work with others to develop themselves. Encourage others to observe you and welcome their feedback, or video your lessons and be your own critic. Just as we tell many of our pupils that we learn from our mistakes, if we don't try something then we might never know how successful it could have been. So my advice is start now. Choose a few of the ideas we have discussed in the book and try them. Remember, practice makes perfect!

Finally, I conclude the book with a checklist covering each key area, which can be used when you visualise and plan your lesson or when you review your lesson, and I wish you every success in becoming an outstanding mathematics teacher.

Planning

- Have I effectively sequenced my lesson with the end point in mind? Do I know where I want my learners to be and how they are going to get there?

- Have I connected the learning?

- Am I aware of any special educational needs and does my plan incorporate them?

- Do I know whether there are going to be any other adults (such as teaching assistants) in my classroom and have I liaised with the member of staff prior to the lesson?
- Does my plan highlight literacy (e.g. key words) and numeracy opportunities?
- Have I planned for the effective use of technology and pre-checked that it works?
- Does my lesson provoke interest?

Learning outcomes

- Have I communicated learning outcomes with the class at a suitable point in the lesson?
- Are outcomes relevant to the specific learners in the group and do they provide appropriate challenge?
- Have I used Bloom's taxonomy as a guide to writing the outcomes?
- Do they enable measurable progress?
- Have I highlighted any key skills that are addressed in the lesson?
- Have I highlighted key vocabulary?

Start of the lesson

- Have I used bell work as appropriate?
- Have I used a challenging Big Question?
- Do I have an engaging starter activity?
- Does the starter connect the learning?
- Does it allow me to be aware of the starting point for every learner (base-lining/benchmarking)?
- Have I assessed and reviewed the starter activity (self-assessment, peer assessment or whole-class assessment) and are pupils aware of their 'starting level'?
- Have I addressed any misconceptions?

Main body of the lesson

- Is the main well 'chunked'?
- Am I facilitating/activating learning and promoting independence?

- Am I regularly using assessment for learning strategies to demonstrate progress and addressing misconceptions?
- Do I use a variety of activities?
- Do I promote a climate for learning?
- Have I contextualised learning and linked to real-life scenarios or used a rich task?
- Have I planned for collaborative learning?
- Have I planned for independent learning?
- Do I promote choice?

Differentiation

- Have I catered for different learning styles (visual, auditory, kinaesthetic or any combination)?
- Have I provided different types of activity?
- How are pupils allocated to these activities? Are they driving their own learning (self-differentiation)?
- What type/types of differentiation have I used?
- Have I planned for differentiation through questioning?
- Have I thought through any groupings (e.g. range of abilities or similar ability groupings and roles within the group)?

Questioning

- Have I adopted a 'hands-down' approach?
- Has every pupil in the class answered at least one question?
- Have I used an appropriate wait time before responding?
- Have I used basketball questioning to develop learning and build concepts?
- Do I encourage pupils to ask questions to develop their learning?
- Am I utilising Bloom's taxonomy to support higher-order thinking skills?
- Am I challenging pupils through questioning?

Assessment for learning and consolidation

- Am I regularly consolidating the learning and linking to outcomes?
- Are pupils driving their own learning?

- Are pupils able to tell me the 'next step' in their learning?
- What type of assessment/assessments for learning techniques have I used?
- Have I used self-assessment or peer assessment?
- How has assessment impacted on learning?

Final assessment activity (plenary)

- Does the plenary allow for demonstration of progress?
- Have I made sure that the plenary is not just more of the same but challenges thinking further?
- Is the plenary open or closed?
- Have I referred back to the learning outcomes or asked pupils to determine the lesson outcomes?
- Have I reviewed the Big Question?
- Are pupils able to reflect on their learning?
- How do I know?
- How do pupils know if they have made progress and can they identify the progress they have made?

Climate for learning

- Am I creating a positive environment?
- Have I welcomed pupils by name and greeted them with a smile?
- Am I managing behaviour consistently and in a positive manner?
- Do I have high expectations of all pupils and communicate these effectively?
- Have I liaised with teaching assistants?
- Have I created a stimulating learning environment through the use of displays?
- Have I thought about the seating plan and layout to suit the activities to be used in the lesson?
- Do pupils leave the lesson with a sense of success and achievement?

References

Works cited

Anderson, L. W. & Krathwohl, D. R. (eds) (2001) *A taxonomy for learning, teaching and assessing: A revision of Bloom's taxonomy of educational objectives (complete edition)*, New York: Longman.

Black, P., Harrison, C., Lee, C., Marshall, B. & William, D. (2003) *Assessment for learning: Putting it into practice*, Maidenhead: Open University Press.

Bloom, B. S. & Krathwohl, D. R. (1956) *Taxonomy of educational objectives: The classification of educational goals, by a committee of college and university examiners; Handbook 1: Cognitive domain*, New York: Longman.

Cotton, K. (1988) *Classroom questioning*, School Improvement Research Series, Portland, OR: Education Northwest, available online at http://educationnorthwest.org/resource/825 (accessed May 2013).

Levin, T. & Long, R. (1981) *Effective instruction*, Alexandria, VA: Association for Supervision and Curriculum Development.

OFSTED (2012a) *Mathematics: made to measure*, available online at www.ofsted.gov.uk/resources/110159 (accessed October 2012).

OFSTED (2012b) *Supplementary subject-specific guidance for mathematics, 30th October 2012*, available online at www.ofsted.gov.uk/resources/generic-grade-descriptors-and-supplementary-subject-specific-guidance-for-inspectors-making-judgements, Ref 201 00015 (accessed October 2012).

Schultz, L. (2005) *Bloom's taxonomy*, Old Dominion University, available online at www.odu.edu/educ/llschult/blooms_taxonomy.htm.

Wiliam, D. & Black, P. (1998) *Inside the black box: Raising standards through classroom assessment*, London: GL Assessment Ltd.

Electronic resources

The Frog, *Frog connects schools around the World*, posted 15th December 2011, http://blog.frogtrade.com/2011/12/15/frog-connects-schools-around-the-world (accessed 20th November 2012).

LTHC Task, http://nrich.maths.org/7701 (accessed 15th November 2012).

Maths and Sport, http://sport.maths.org (accessed 30th September 2012).

Motivate, *Maths enrichment for schools*, http://motivate.maths.org/content/MultiMediaResources (accessed 30th September 2012).

NRICH, *Multiplication tables: Matching cards*, University of Cambridge, http://nrich.maths.org/1252 (accessed 12th October 2012).

NRICH, *Coordinate Challenge*, University of Cambridge, http://nrich.maths.org/5038 (accessed 12th October 2012).

UNC Center for Teaching and Learning, *Writing objectives using Bloom's Taxonomy*, http://teaching.uncc.edu/articles-books/best-practice-articles/goals-objectives/writing-objectives-using-blooms-taxonomy (accessed 16th November 2012).

Websites referenced for resources

All these were accessed in October 2012.

http://hotpot.uvic.ca
http://plus.maths.org
http://sport.maths.org
http://teaching.unac.edu
www.atm.org.uk
www.docs.google.com
www.dynamicgeometry.com
www.geogebra.org
www.mymaths.co.uk
www.ncetm.org.uk
www.nrich.org
www.problempictures.co.uk
www.schoolsworld.tv
www.statistics.gov.uk
www.STEMnot.org
www.suffolkmaths.co.uk
www.teacherled.com
www.teachersmedia.co.uk
www.tes.co.uk
www.thefutureschannel.com

Index

Index

Index